Democracy
—IN—
CUBA?

Democracy
— IN —
CUBA?

Carlos Méndez Tovar

Editorial **José Martí**

Original title in Spanish: *¿Democracia en Cuba?*
Translated by: *Angela Todd, Mercedes Guillot and Lori Nordstrom*
Edited by: *María Dolores Piñeda, Rosa María Marrero and Fernando Nápoles Tapia*
Cover design by: *J. A. Mompeller*
Electronic composition by: *Beatriz Roussó*

First Spanish-language edition (5,000 copies): November, 1995.
Second Spanish-language edition (3,000 copies): April, 1997.
First English-language edition (5,000 copies): April, 1997.

INSTITUTO CUBANO DEL LIBRO
EDITORIAL JOSÉ MARTÍ
Publicaciones en Lenguas Extranjeras
Apartado postal 4208, La Habana 10400, Cuba

ISBN 959-09-0103-4

This book travels courtesy of Cubana Airlines.

To my wife Mercedes
To my children Carlos V.
Marielita
Arnold
To my granddaughters Yulia
Gabriela

CONTENTS

Cuba . . . changed from security threat to political curiosity.

—The New York Times, July 16, 1993

INTRODUCTION

The accelerated development of science and technology in the contemporary world has exerted an influence on all spheres of life, including communications. To a major extent, this has determined that themes and concepts that a few decades ago were handled almost exclusively by specialists and scholars are now, in practice, managed with varying accuracy and according to individual interests and capacity by the overwhelming majority of human beings, and even by those who have no direct relationship with the mass media. Thus, concepts such as democracy, civil rights, human rights and others are used daily, although not always accurately, by millions of men and women in the world.

On the other hand, the mass media, which are steadily becoming more sophisticated and effective, lie in the hands of powerful consortia responding to the major powers that dominate the contemporary world. For that reason it is not surprising that the media serve to shape criteria and create opinions that favor the interests of those powers.

Right from the triumph of the Cuban Revolution, in January 1959, Cuba has been the object of heavily concentrated fire from newspapers, magazines, radio, television, cinema, books, etc. Millions of words and images on certain occasions and total silence at other times, have cultivated disinformation concerning Cuban realities for over 30 years.

A great many visitors to Cuba, even those with a positive attitude towards the island, have discovered on arrival that they didn't really know what it was like, what was happening, or how life is lived in this Caribbean country.

Is there democracy in Cuba? Do non-governmental organizations exist there? How do Cubans live? Are elections held? These are some of the many questions regularly asked.

Cuba's potential for confronting the avalanche of biased and distorted information spread by the communications transnationals is obviously limited. Nevertheless, a superhuman effort has been and is being made to try to give the world a genuine image of what has been going on for more than 36 years in this country.

These reflections lead us to see this book from José Martí Publishers as a useful effort in the battle to promote awareness of current Cuban realities. There are many other publications dealing with various aspects covered here, but its usefulness lies precisely in the fact that its author, Méndez Tovar, has managed to summarize and present a global vision of them all in one concise volume. This synthesis, however, has been preceded by arduous investigative research. A voluminous quantity of news dispatches, speeches and documents have passed through the author's diligent hands, and held up to the light of his own experiences in other countries, particularly in Latin America.

The reader has been given the opportunity to understand and compare with his or her own experiences aspects of prime importance in the life of any society, because it can be stated without a doubt that basic human rights in Cuba are not only established in a legal document but also guaranteed by the state: the right to work, to education, to medical care, to culture; the right to a life free of racial or gender discrimination; the right to make decisions about and participate in the running of the state; the right to organize, and to train for the nation's defense.

One theme in particular is handled with helpful detail: the Cuban electoral system. Tovar's meticulous explanation of the electoral process allows one to understand that Cuban citizens are not passive beings limited to voting for people who have actually been designated by groups and parties, but rather that they are the ones who decide on the candidates.

This book is not restricted to the Cuban situation. In a concise yet inclusive manner it gives us a contemporary panorama of countries like the United States that attempt to style themselves as the leaders of democracy and the defenders of human rights. With equal conciseness, it presents the truth about the aggressive attitude maintained by every U.S. administration since 1959 and the violation of human rights that is part of the unjust economic blockade to which the island has been subjected for several decades.

Without a doubt, those who wish to learn about Cuba from both an internal and external point of view, who wish to comprehend the real nature of the Cuban Revolution and understand why the Cuban people firmly maintain their positions and are prepared to defend their gains and keep to the path they have chosen, will find this book a valuable tool.

NIURKA ESCALANTE COLÁS

PART ONE

SOME REFLECTIONS ON THE CONCEPT
OF DEMOCRACY

*We hold these truths to be self-evident, that all men are
created equal, that they are endowed by their Creator with
certain unalienable rights, that among these are life,
liberty and the pursuit of happiness.*

—Declaration of Independence of the United States of America

On numerous occasions some Ibero-American heads of state
have shown a sustained concern for Cuba's fate and consequently
are in the habit of making recommendations and proposals to
the Cuban president to agree to a "democratic opening" in order
to improve relations with the U.S. government.

International news agencies disseminate the U.S. viewpoint,
according to which the Cuban people are hungry for democracy. However, the Cuban media assure the world that an authentic democracy is flourishing and being consolidated in the
country.

Contradictory opinions from one side or another, attacks,
explanations and, in the end, doubts have been the order of the
day for the overwhelming majority of the planet's inhabitants
who lack the resources to find out for themselves what is happening in Cuba. Cuba is a concern, an unknown for millions of
human beings of all creeds and political positions.

It is very difficult to gain, from a distance, an objective image of something as complex as a socioeconomic system. In
order to acquire a vision that comes as close as possible to the
reality, the only practical approach is to have some direct con-

tact with Cuban events, in addition to using information from such internationally recognized organizations as the World Health Organization (WHO), the United Nations Children's Fund (UNICEF), the Pan American Health Organization (PAHO), the United Nations Food and Agriculture Organization (FAO), the United Nations Development Program (UNDP), the United Nations Educational, Scientific and Cultural Organization (UNESCO), and so on. This information would provide for serious and interesting research for those whose possibilities of traveling to the Caribbean island are limited.

To ensure that sympathies or antipathies, or the employment of preestablished recipes or dogmas, do not contaminate or detract from the final research results, I have turned to official documents, reliable statistics confirmed by the aforementioned organizations, government programs and their application, and objective results; in short, all the methods used by social scientists.

Let's begin by defining democracy. A magazine bearing this title, published by the United States Information and Cultural Service, can help us to understand it. In an article headlined "A Definition of Democracy", it informs us that:

> The dictionary defines democracy as "government by the people, in which supreme power is conferred on the people and is directly exercised by them, or by agents chosen by them by means of a free electoral system." In the words of Abraham Lincoln, democracy is the government "of the people, by the people and for the people."[1]

Some dictionaries explain the word's semantic origin: "Democracy (from Greek *demokratia;* from *demos*, people; *kratos*, authority). Form of government in which sovereignty is exercised by the people."[2]

---

1. Howard Cincotta. "Definición de democracia" (A Definition of Democracy), in *¿Qué es la democracia?*, 4.
2. *Webster's New Collegiate Dictionary.*

Other dictionaries tell us: "Democracy. A political doctrine favoring popular intervention in the political government of a state."[3]

Any democrat would confirm that the principle of democracy implies recognition of the freedom and equal rights of citizens and the principle of the subordination of the minority to the majority.

Strangely enough, not everybody claiming to be a democrat has the same opinion regarding concepts as significant as equal rights, freedom, subordination of the minority to the majority, popular intervention in the political government of the state, human rights, and so on.

For example, let's look at the U.S. magazine *¿Qué es la democracia?*, which presents the official view of the U.S. government regarding human rights issues:

> Recently it has been observed, particularly in the case of international organizations, that the list of basic human rights is tending to grow longer. To the essential liberties of freedom of expression and equal treatment before the law, these groups have added the right to employment, to education, to one's own culture or nationality and to decent standards of living....
>
> But when such benefits proliferate as rights, there is a tendency to devalue the significance of basic civil and human rights.[4]

The U.S. style of democracy has these rights perfectly well defined, and they are laid out in a table in the aforementioned magazine:

---

3. José Alemany y Bolufer. *Nuevo diccionario de la lengua española* (New Dictionary of the Spanish Language).
4. Howard Cincotta. "Derechos" (Rights), op. cit., 12.

Basic Human Rights
- Freedom of speech, expression and of the press.
- Freedom of religion.
- Freedom to meet and associate.
- The right to receive the same protection from the law.
- The right to due judicial process and to a fair trial.[5]

In the view of millions of people, when human rights have a maximum limit, they become abstract concepts of no use to anybody. These persons add that the greater the number of rights enjoyed by a human being, the happier that person feels. Thus, if political, social, civil and economic rights—signified by the right to work, to education, to health care, to sports, to recreation, to culture, to the integral development of a person's capacities, to respect for personal integrity, to elect and be elected regardless of wealth or membership of any political party, and to enjoy these rights irrespective of race, gender, origin or religion—were added to those listed by the U.S. magazine, then human beings would undoubtedly feel more complete, given the prospect of their free and total self-realization. This is in complete contrast to the U.S. publication's argument concerning the supposed devaluation of the meaning of basic civil and human rights.

One could then run the risk of adding something else to the aforementioned criteria for democracy, by stating that it should be an *attitude towards life* (of both those who govern and those governed), since it is a doctrine that favors popular intervention in the political government of the state. This presupposes more power in the hands of the people and a similarity of interests between the government and those governed, all of which brings us very close to Lincoln's definition of democracy.

Global consensus on some of the points previously covered does not exist, which means that we must go ahead and observe, compare and draw our own conclusions.

5. Ibid, 11.

One of the parameters used to measure the democratic nature of a system is so-called universal suffrage or free elections. Using this mechanism one can see if the minority accedes to the majority. Therefore, if we are to attempt to grasp the characteristics of the Cuban socioeconomic model, our research has to be directed towards ascertaining whether the Cuban government respects the democratic principles of equal rights, freedom, the subordination of the minority to the majority, the holding of free elections, affording people ample space in the political government of the state. Also highly significant is whether a Constitution exists and by whom and in what manner it was drawn up. The results obtained in an investigation along these lines can be compared with other known systems and will provide a response for those who want to know what goes on in Cuba.

LITERACY AND EDUCATION

Morality and intelligence are our first needs.
—Simón Bolívar

There is no social equality without equality of culture.
—José Martí

If we adhere to the spirit of the letter "equality of the rights of citizens", the elemental right to learn how to read and write is inalienable. The Cuban system has absolutely no objection to including it within that category, since equality of rights cannot exist if there is no equality of opportunity, and equality of opportunity is impossible in the case of an illiterate person.

Cuba's commitment to provide this right to all its citizens is reflected in Havana's Literacy Museum where, apart from records and documents of its literacy campaign—a process that eradicated illiteracy in just one year—it presents the constitutional right of all citizens to become literate.

Article 39, clause b) of that guiding document of Cuban society states:

> Education is a function of the state and is free of charge. It is based on the conclusions and contributions made by science and on the close relationship between study and life, work and production.
>
> The state maintains a broad scholarship system for students and provides workers with multiple opportunities to study to be able to attain the highest possible levels of knowledge and skills.
>
> The law establishes the integration and structure of the national system of education and the extent of compul-

sory education and defines the minimum level of general education that every citizen should acquire. . . .[6]

In response to the logical question as to whether Cuba fulfills what is written in the Constitution, Cubans leave the answer to UNESCO and UNICEF. In addition to confirming that this is the case, these organizations praise Cuban achievements in this sphere, because they were not limited to simply eradicating illiteracy; newly literate persons were encouraged to continue their studies and many have reached advanced levels. Most importantly, a pedagogic-educational structure was established to prevent this social problem from reappearing. The Literacy Museum preserves the traces of an inhumane past unknown to current generations, but one that continues to be a terrible social disease, without any prospect of cure, in other countries of the Americas.

When the Cuban government takes pride in stating that it has eradicated illiteracy, it means exactly that: illiteracy has been extirpated, rooted out. Nowadays, nobody wants to "escape" from compulsory education up to the ninth grade.

The pedagogic-educational structure does not exclude children with disabilities (blindness, visual impairment, deaf-mutism, or other kinds of learning difficulties) from its classrooms. These children are provided with special schools, staffed by specially trained personnel, rigorously selected in terms of their professional, vocational and humane qualities and grouped in multidisciplinary teams.

Nor has the Cuban system turned its back on orphaned children, referred to here as "children of the nation". The special centers created for these children are a genuinely humane achievement, an unassailable triumph, and a source of tremendous pride. The children in these schools are lovingly cared for and given special attention by the staff. In this way, the Cuban

6. *Constitution of the Republic of Cuba.* Editora Política publishers.

model has eliminated the Dantesque tableau —as witnessed in our countries—of millions of children abandoned to their fate, wandering the streets and living off public charity. These children become corrupted, turning to prostitution, drug abuse and trafficking, without the slightest hope of a decent life. In Cuba, homeless, abandoned, or exploited children do not exist.

If equal rights begin with equality of opportunity, then they can be described as real and not simply theoretical in a country where children don't have to sell their labor to acquire school supplies, food or transportation to school, because these are guaranteed.

That is the first striking reality that we find in this Caribbean island. For those of us who are not Cuban, statements made by U.S. Vice President Al Gore to the Canadian magazine *Computer Current*, published by *Today/Tomorrow*, come as no surprise; the second-in-charge at the White House laments: "It's disgraceful that we have this level of illiteracy, countries like Cuba put us to shame when it comes to this problem...."[7]

Neither is it surprising that a country like Venezuela which exports 2.5 million barrels of oil per day and has only 20 million inhabitants should exhibit a reality such as this: "Some 2.7 million children, approximately 50% of the country's school age population, are outside of the Venezuelan preschool education system, according to Ministry of Education estimates. The ministry has plans to put emergency plans into action."[8]

According to official figures detailed in the Spanish edition of the *World Almanac 1994*, published in the United States, 4.5% of the population in Lincoln's homeland cannot read or

7. "Índice de alfabetizados en Cuba, vergüenza para Estados Unidos" (Literacy Rate in Cuba, Humiliation for the United States), in *Granma* daily, February 24, 1994, 4. (Retranslated from Spanish.)
8. "Crisis educacional en Venezuela" (Educational Crisis in Venezuela), in *Granma* daily, March 3, 1994, 4.

write.[9] In other words, over 11 million U.S. citizens are illiterate, although unofficial figures indicate 30 million, without counting the undereducated. A figure higher than the total number of inhabitants in Cuba, with that elemental right denied to them.

Nor does this March 1993 AFP news dispatch come as a surprise:

> New Yorkers are but a fraction of those adrift in U.S. cities, where a million minors leave home every year, for different reasons. Of this total, 40% are black, 30% Hispanic, 25% white and 5% Asian. Five percent are HIV positive....

> Every night a blue truck belonging to a humanitarian organization drives through the streets of New York looking for some of the 20,000 children who, thanks to drugs or prostitution, survive on their own in the largest city in the richest country in the world.[10]

We are in complete agreement with Vice President Gore: it is humiliating and shameful that, on the threshold of the 21st century, a country that has always prided itself on being an exemplary democracy should have such a lamentable reality, humiliating both for those who suffer it and those who propitiate it.

The contrast with Cuban education is starker when other data are revealed:

- Half of Cuban children under six years of age receive educational attention.

- The Cuban model has produced over 500,000 university graduates and hundreds of thousands of technical students.

- It has 200,000 teachers and professors (many of whom

9. *World Almanac 1994*, p. 302.
10. AFP, New York, March 4, 1993.

have university degrees and postgraduate studies).

- It has 11,000 scientists, the vast majority of whom are young.

- The education budget for 1994 was in excess of 1.3 billion pesos.

- Free education has been maintained for 34 years.[11]

The per capita of students is the highest in the world.

> Today Cuba has the highest literacy rate in the Americas, and one of the highest in the world, with 98.2% of its population having received at least an 8th grade education, according to UNESCO endorsed figures. It has achieved the highest index of teachers per capita in the world, with one teacher per 37 inhabitants. [12]

In spite of these premises, it seems premature to talk of equality, because although the absence of illiterate persons affords equal opportunities to all citizens, this on its own is not enough. Other human rights must be enjoyed to accept that this is a genuine democracy.

11. René Márquez Castro. "Rediseño de la política social cubana" (Cuban Social Policy Redesigned), in *Bohemia* magazine, November 11, 1994, 16.
12. Ibid.

Table 1
Population and Illiteracy (%)
(the Americas)

Country	Population	Illiterates	Illiteracy (%)*
Argentina	32, 608, 680	1, 532, 608	4.7
Bolivia	6, 344, 300	1, 427, 468	22.5
Brazil	153, 322, 000	29, 231, 000	19.0
Chile	13, 386, 000	883, 000	6.6
Colombia	33, 613, 000	4, 470, 529	13.3
Costa Rica	3, 064, 000	220, 608	7.2
Cuba**	10, 736, 000	-	0.0
Dominican Rep.	7, 313, 000	1, 221, 271	16.7
Ecuador	10, 851, 000	1, 504, 842	14.2
El Salvador	5, 376, 000	1, 451, 520	27.0
Guatemala	10, 029, 414	4, 503, 206	44.9
Haiti	6, 625, 000	3, 113, 750	47.0
Honduras	5, 265, 000	1, 416, 285	26.9

Country	Population	Illiterates	Illiteracy (%)**
Mexico	87, 836 000	11, 155 162	12.7
Nicaragua	3, 999 000	5,20 000	13.0
Peru	22, 914 606	2, 451 862	10.7
Puerto Rico	3, 551 000	3,87 059	10.9
United States	252, 688 000	11, 370 000	4.5
Uruguay	3, 112 000	1,18 256	3.8
Venezuela	20, 266 000	2, 411 654	11.9

SOURCE: Compiled by the author from data taken from the Spanish edition of the *World Almanac 1994*, printed in the United States of America by St. Ives, Inc. 2025 McKinley St., Hollywood, Fl., America Publishers, S.A., 1993.

* These statistics are from 1990, except for Puerto Rico (1980), Nicaragua (1985), Brazil (1988), the United States (1989), and Peru and the Dominican Republic (1991).

** Cuba was declared free of illiteracy in 1962.

SPORTS

Before the triumph of the Cuban Revolution in 1959, the country's national anthem was never heard at the medal-awarding ceremonies of Olympic, world or even regional games. In the Pan American and Central American Games, Cuban successes were so discreet that one could safely assume that sports weren't practiced in Cuba. Just occasionally in baseball, thanks to the individual efforts of one athlete or another, were some minor personal successes achieved.

With the new system, Cuban sports started on a course that would ascend to vertiginous heights. At every event, whether at regional, world or Olympic level, the dignified performance of Cuban athletes led to so much repetition of the anthem that those of other Third World countries were barely heard. To give the reader an idea, in the Havana '91 Pan American Games, the Cuban national anthem was played 140 times, ten times more than that of the United States.

Cuba, surprisingly, gained fourteenth place in the 1972 Munich Olympics, in which 122 countries participated. Four years later, in Montreal 1976, the island climbed to eighth place.[13]

For reasons of principle, Cuban athletes absented themselves from the Olympic Games for 12 years. They reappeared in Barcelona 1992 where they reached fifth place among 172 countries, only superceded by four of the world's biggest powers. This is reflected in the following table:

13. Data taken from Conrado Martínez Corona, then president of the National Institute of Sports, Physical Education and Recreation (INDER). "Compartimos con nuestro pueblo la alegría de habernos ubicado en quinto puesto" (We Share with Our People the Joy of Winning 5th Place), in *Granma* daily, August 12, 1992, 5.

Table 2
Population and Gold Medals Per Million Inhabitants
(Barcelona'92 Olympics)

	Population	Gold	Silver	Bronze	Total	Gold medals per million inhabitants
CIS	260 million	45	38	29	112	0.16
USA	250 million	37	34	37	108	0.14
Ger.	80 million	33	21	28	82	0.41
China	1200 million	16	22	16	54	0.01
Cuba	11 million	14	6	11	31	1.27

SOURCE: Compiled by the author from data taken from *Gramma* daily, August 12, 1992, 5.

As indicated, the table compares gold medals per million inhabitants, which ranks Cuba as world leader. The Latin American countries alone have over 450 million inhabitants and gained just two gold medals; Cuba, with 11 million, obtained seven times more. If we add those gained by the Ibero-American countries, we shall see that Cuba won 50% of all the medals in that group of nations. Latin America, the Caribbean and Canada combined managed only eight as opposed to Cuba's 14.

Cubans are proud of their achievements, but regret that other Third World countries lack the resources and opportunities that would enable their populations to enjoy a right as important as the practice of sports.

Equal opportunities ensure that nobody is excluded or marginalized. Since 1989, Cuba has maintained its position as Latin American champion of the Games for the Blind and Visually Impaired. The 14 athletes who comprised the Cuban delegation in this category to the 5th Latin American Games, held in São Paulo, Brazil, from September 19-27, 1994, returned home with 37 gold medals, nine silver and one bronze, earning them top place overall.[14]

Cuba also took second place in the first International Mental Health Olympics, held in Puerto Rico, September 1994, winning 60 medals (24 gold, 24 silver and 12 bronze) with only 18 athletes, as well as being awarded the vice presidency of the Mental Health Sports Organization.

These laurels were all won for the country by the Havana Psychiatric Hospital, whose director, Dr. Bernabé Ordaz, said:

> The fact that physical exercise and sports activities occupy a central place in our patients' individual and group rehabilitation programs is in line with scientifically proven

14. Hortensia Torres. "Cuba campeón latinoamericano en Juegos para Ciegos y Débiles Visuales" (Cuba, Latin American Champion in Games for the Blind and Visually Impaired), in *Granma* daily, September 29, 1994, 3.

knowledge of the positive influence on the patient of these activities, from the physical, psychological and social points of view.[15]

Achieving all those successes, and the fact that out of the 192-member Cuban delegation to Barcelona, 172 athletes from this small island ranked among the top eight in the world, requires—at least—a logical or rational explanation, because we are looking at a rare phenomenon. It's impossible to attribute those spectacular triumphs to genetic or fortuitous causes. At the same time, it's also apparent that this is a reflection of the undeniable merits of the Cuban model, which has much to contribute to other countries.

Research indicates that the secret lies in the strict fulfillment of the rights that Article 52 of the Constitution guarantees to all citizens:

> Everybody has the right to physical education, sports and recreation. Enjoyment of this right is assured by including the teaching and practice of physical education and sports in the curricula of he national education system; and by the broad nature of the instruction and means placed at the service of the people, which makes possible the practice of sports and recreation on a mass basis.[16]

To continue with this undertaking, in one of Cuba's most critical years in economic terms (1994), a total of 102.8 million pesos was devoted to the sector.

Every sports medal gained by Cuba is supported by a massive infrastructure, with nothing improvised. The big secret lies in mass participation from childhood, requiring the investment of several million pesos every year to finance the con-

---

15. Rolando Valdés Marín. "Ganan 60 medallas pacientes del Hospital Psiquiátrico" (Psychiatric Hospital Patients Win 60 Medals), in *Juventud Rebelde* weekly, October 2, 1994, 14.

16. *Constitution of the Republic of Cuba*, loc. cit.

struction of sports facilities, to manufacture and import equipment, to train instructors, coaches and referees, to build schools, to contract foreign specialists, to send athletes to other countries for competitions and training, etc.

In general, the efforts Cuban athletes have to make in order to win each and every medal are not known. They are forced to compete under unequal conditions, as much due to the particular circumstances of a besieged country as to the psychological disadvantages under which the island's athletes compete in foreign countries, given the U.S. government's undemocratic practice of subjecting Cuban athletes to tremendous pressure, such as offering them huge sums of money to defect. In addition, every possible obstacle is put in the way of the Cuban delegation to prevent it from reaching events on time, such as denying or delaying visas when meets are held in the United States or in Puerto Rico, along with other unimaginable pressures.

For example, Notimex reported: "The International Shooting Union (ISU) could withdraw the hosting of the 1995 World Cup from the United States, because of State Department hindrances on 500 shooters traveling to Cuba during the touring stages."[17]

Cuban athletes demonstrate an impressive degree of patriotic pride by turning down tempting sums—sometimes in the million mark—and have a low regard for those who believe that dignity has a price. Even greater than the number of actual medals won is the number of such medals of dignity and honor brought home by many other Cubans besides these athletes.

Cubans say that the greatest triumph of the Barcelona Olympics was that the entire delegation of over 200 returned to Cuba,

17. "Impide EE.UU. traslado de 500 deportistas de varios países a Cuba" (U.S. Hampers Cuba Tour of 500 Athletes from Various Countries), in *Granma* daily, April 20, 1994, 3.

in spite of pressures brought to bear on both athletes and trainers by U.S. agents, in attempts to persuade them to defect. This occurred at the hardest moment of the economic crisis facing Cuba as a result of the U.S. economic blockade.

Researchers have to concede that a cruel and discriminatory policy that damages the development of sports doesn't correspond to democratic ideals, much less so in a country that views the healthy exercise of this practice as an inalienable right of all its people.

A realistic analysis of the figures leads to the conclusion that those 172 athletes who placed among the top eight in the world, were the cream of a reduced segment of society, given that this is the age of competitive high performance sports. This gives us an idea of Cuba's potential reserves since all members of its population—and especially its youth—have access to the practice of sports.

CULTURE

To be cultured is the only way to be free.
—José Martí

The cultural heritage of all of humanity has been enriched by contributions from Cuba, encouraged by a high budget allotted to this sphere (164.1 million pesos in 1994).

For the Cuban citizen, classical ballet has long ceased to be an activity enjoyed by an elite. The renowned Cuban School of Ballet offers the island's privileged public an opportunity to enjoy the best and most select of the genre on a universal scale, in periodically organized festivals. We're not the first nor will we be the last to be amazed at the derisory sum of two to five pesos paid by Cubans to attend a gala that would cost up to hundreds of dollars in Europe or the United States. Widescale participation is the common denominator for both the enjoyment and practice of this activity. The country's various schools are open to anybody with the necessary talent and interest. The most prestigious critics and renowned artists agree that a new and highly significant school of ballet has developed in Cuba, from which there is much to be learned.

In the visual arts, a young and vigorous Cuban movement has successfully forged an individual style, characterized by a high degree of talent and, once more, by its mass appeal. The influential Cuban visual arts movement includes many young artists. The Havana Biennial is renowned throughout the world and attended by a public eager to increase its cultural wealth.

A steadily growing number of Cuban artists are expanding their country's cultural horizons and gaining a footing in other countries. This gives their work an international character while reinforcing their Cuban and Latin American identity. Many of these talented young people hail from rural areas and are the fruit of a conscious and systematic promotion of the arts.

The island is also a venue for guitar, theater and cinema festivals where the greatest international talents compete. In Cuba they find receptivity and a creative and participative enthusiasm, given that a great deal of experience goes into the programming and organizing of these events. Audiences at these festivals grow more demanding as their levels of artistic appreciation heighten.

The country also has an active participation in several overseas international events. Cuban successes in international scenarios are well-known, ranging from piano and guitar performances to the cinema, theater, popular music, painting, drawing, sculpture, and so on.

These successes are not plucked out of the air. They are the result of a concern for culture that begins with a considerable state funding and continues with painstaking efforts at infrastructural and organizational levels. This cultural development has been achieved by building schools, establishing hundreds of cultural centers, manufacturing and importing thousands of musical instruments, hiring and inviting teachers and artists, training tens of thousands of art instructors (Cuba has the highest number of them per capita in the world), participating in competitions, events and festivals, and publishing literature and teaching materials. This is what is involved in fulfilling the words of the Cuban Constitution that define culture as an inalienable right of working people, who enjoy it from childhood, or from the moment that human beings begin to develop their capacities.

The country has a strong and wide-ranging literary movement, regularly fortified by new talent, the consequence of a considerable investment of time, dedication and much love. It should be sufficient to note that the most important universal classics have been reprinted in Cuba and sold at a subsidized rate, commencing in the same year as the Revolution, 1959, with Cervantes' *Don Quixote*. For many years, visitors to the island have been taken aback by the quality content and low cost of books. To be able to read any classic for 70 to 90 cents or one peso is a genuine privilege. National contests are also held to encourage literary creativity.

The country organizes periodic book fairs. In 1989, the per capita publication and importing of books was higher than that of any other Third World country. A simple mathematical operation indicates that the number of titles published per 100,000 inhabitants in the United States is equal to those published in Cuba. (See Table 5 at the end of this chapter.)

Millions of volumes are stored in Cuban libraries, spread throughout every city and town. Traveling libraries have also been established to transport culture to the country's remotest areas.

The prestigious Casa de las Américas Prize, which carries considerable weight in international intellectual spheres, particularly in Latin America, is integrationalist in character and was created with the express objective of strengthening Latin American identity. For that reason, the spectrum of participants is regularly expanded, so as to give space to ethnic minorities using their language of origin.

Within the last three years, two Cuban writers have been awarded prestigious international prizes: the Spanish Cervantes Award and the Mexican Juan Rulfo Award. Two other Cuban authors jointly received the Tirso de Molina Prize, the most important Ibero-American theater award, presented every year in Spain.

Cuba has not only developed a quality cinema, but has promoted this artistic genre throughout Latin America. The Cuban Film Institute (ICAIC) organizes the internationally acclaimed annual Festival of New Latin American Cinema, in which the best productions of the continent can be enjoyed for a mere two pesos. The Latin American Film School is also based in Cuba.

All Cuban cultural activities achieve a harmonious combination of the international and national in order to enrich the population's aesthetic values.

Another aspect of Cuban culture can be found in its museums. These have proliferated throughout the country, and the care and attention given them by the population as a whole has sustained the nation's and the world's historic, artistic and cultural heritage.

A country in which education, culture, work, sports, health care and social security are rights held by the population as a whole is more equitable, more humane and, of course, more democratic than one in which only one sector of it can enjoy those vital rights.

It should be added that the economic blockade—which the United States also describes as a low intensity war—is not only financial, commercial and economic, but has the further stated objective of undermining patriotic values and Cuban national identity and culture. In order to preserve these values, Cubans place ever greater emphasis on the study of their country's history and the thinking of Martí and Bolívar.

The following figures reflect Cuban development levels in this important sphere.

Table 3
Current Statistics on Cuban Culture

Films and videos

Feaure films	8
Shorts	31
Newsreels	26
Movie theaters	507
Premiers	68 (less than in 1989)
Showings	377, 260
Attendance	19, 756, 000 spectators
16-mm movie equipment	572
Showings	278, 000
Attendance	15, 700, 000 spectators
Video rooms	223
Showings	101, 800

Book publishing and libraries

Books published	1, 858 titles
Print run	45, 376, 700 copies
Income	15, 400, 000 pesos
Public libraries	338
Users	5, 900, 000 persons
Books borrowed	8, 000, 000 copies

Music

Record production	1, 167, 000 units
Copies of sheet music	45, 000
String instruments (manufactured)	1, 400
Percussion instruments (manufactured)	2, 500
Cassettes manufactured (exported)	205, 000

Music performances	45, 400
Attendance	14, 076, 000 persons
Variety shows	1, 144
Attendance	534, 000 persons
Discotheque takings	1, 600, 000 pesos

Theater arts

Theaters	19
Theater halls	27
Performances	6, 400
Takings	880, 000 pesos
Attendance	970, 000 persons
Dance performances	882
Attendance	283, 200 persons

Circus

Tents	5
Performances	1, 114
Attendance	376, 000 persons
Takings	2, 200, 000 pesos

Visual arts

Galleries	117
Exhibitions	933
Visitors	1, 500, 000 persons

SOURCE: Compiled by the author from data taken from *Algunos datos sobre la gestión cultural actual*. (Some Facts on Current Cultural Activities), (Havana: Ministry of Culture, 1991), 19-20.

Table 4

Community Cultural Institutions
(1980-1990)

	1980	1985	1990
Museums	79	245	255
Libraries	196	312	339
Community art centers	132	232	271
35-mm movie theaters	515	510	535
Art galleries	28	139	117
Theaters and theater halls	48	42	46
Bookstores	252	316	345

SOURCE: *Some Facts on Current Cultural Activities,* 17.

Table 5
Population and Titles Published
(the Americas)

Country	Population	Date	Titles published	Titles published per 100 000 inhabitants
Argentina	32, 608, 680	1987	4,836	25.5
Bolivia	6, 344, 300	1988	447	7.0
Brazil	153, 322, 000	1985	17,648	11.5
Chile	13, 386, 000	1989	2, 350	17.6
Colombia	33, 613, 000	1989	1, 486	4.4
Costa Rica	3, 064, 000	1990	244	8.1
Cuba	10, 736, 000	1989	2, 199	20.5
Dominican Rep.	7, 313, 000	1983	1, 504	20.6
El Salvador	5, 376, 000	1988	15	0.28
Guatemala	10, 029, 414	1983	312	3.1

Haiti	6, 625, 000	1989	271	4.1
Mexico	87, 836, 000	1983	3, 490	3.9
Nicaragua	3, 999, 000	1987	41	1.0
Panama	2, 466, 000	1983	114	4.6
Peru	22, 914, 606	1988	481	2.1
United States	252, 688, 000	1983	51, 058	20.2
Uruguay	3, 112, 000	1989	805	25.9
Venezuela	20, 266, 000	1987	1, 202	5.9

SOURCE: Compiled by the author from data taken from the *World Almanac 1994*, loc. cit.

International Cultural Events Held in Cuba

Ballet Festival (biennial)
International Ballet Course (annual)
Festival of New Latin American Cinema (annual)
Visual Arts Biennial
International Book Fair (biennial)
Theater Festival (biennial)
Monologue and One-Person Show Biennial
Humor Festival (biennial)
Contemporary Music Festival (annual)
Bolero Festival (annual)
Jazz Festival (biennial)
Choir Festival (biennial)
Guitar Festival (biennial)
Light Opera Festival (biennial)
Son Festival (biennial)
Benny Moré Popular Music Festival (biennial, alternating with the *Son* Festival)
Caribbean Culture Festival (annual)
Casa de las Américas Prize (annual)
FIART International Popular Art Festival (biennial)
Dance Festival (annual)
Folklore Festival (started in 1995, future frequency unknown)
Imprint of Spain Festival
Ibero-American Culture Festival (annual)
Cuban Identity Festival (annual)
Contemporary Cuban Art Salon (annual)
Latin American Art Education Conference
Contemporary Dance Workshop (twice yearly)
Folklore Dance Workshop (twice yearly)
Scientific Conference on Art (biennial)
Pro Danza International Ballet Workshop (annual)

WORK

*Work in a socialist society is a right and duty and a source of pride
for every citizen.*
—Article 45 of the Constitution of the Republic of Cuba

After demonstrating Cuba's achievements in such a convincing way, it can also be inferred that the country offers a labor code in line with its achievements in other spheres.

In effect, given the huge chaos within "democratic models" characterized by rampant neoliberalism, the result of laying off millions of workers without any form of social security; compared with the inhumane shock policies implemented by the insatiable ruling classes in the majority of Third World countries so as to make the economic adjustments that will guarantee certain profit levels and, of course, increased personal wealth; in relation to the geometrically progressive increase of poverty and marginality; and given the conditions of slavery facing many workers throughout the world, Cuban labor practices are genuinely humane.

Articles 47 and 48 of the Cuban Constitution read:

> By means of the Social Security System the state assures adequate protection to every worker who is unable to work because of age, illness or disability. . . .

> The state protects, by means of social assistance, senior citizens lacking financial resources or anyone who is unable to work and has no relatives who can help them.[18]

The conquests gained by Cuban workers are among the most advanced in the world. They are the protagonists when legislation regulating their working lives is drawn up.

18. *Constitution of the Republic of Cuba,* loc. cit.

The state also guarantees the right to health and safety at work, by adopting adequate workplace accident and sickness prevention measures. Workers who do find themselves in one of these situations have the right to medical care and a supplementary or retirement pension in cases of temporary or permanent incapacity.

Society as a whole is the defender of workers' rights, but the trade unions have an obligation and a duty to ensure that labor legislation is complied with.

Recently, as a consequence of the shortage of fuel and spare parts, transportation has suffered reductions. Cuban workers have sought various alternatives, one of which is to change jobs with another worker so as to live nearer the workplace.

For those who like figures, one out of every ten Cubans is a pensioner, and more than 11,400 disabled workers are incorporated into productive labor. Moreover, the state distributes 4.3 million pesos daily in pensions and 35.9 million in social assistance.[19]

In relation to this subject, *The Financial Times* newspaper recently stated that U.S. workers are among the most unprotected in the world; only 15.8% of the labor force is unionized and if government employees are excluded from this figure, the percentage falls to less than 12%.[20]

A further significant indicator is that the Cuban work force is the most qualified in the continent.

Clearly, a society in which unemployment doesn't exist and in which all citizens are socially protected by a system that offers them this security is a society in which there is greater social justice.

19. René Márquez Castro. Op. cit., 16, and Silvia Martínez. "Invierte Cuba 4,3 millones de pesos cada 24 horas en la seguridad social" (Cuba Invests 4.3 Million Pesos Every 24 Hours in Social Security), in *Granma* daily, June 10, 1994, 2.
20. Juana Carrasco Martín. "Vericuetos de una manipulación" (The Rough Tracks of Manipulation), in *Bohemia* magazine, March 19, 1993, 49.

WOMEN

When an educated and virtuous woman anoints a work with the sweetness of her affection—that work is invincible.

—José Martí

"The protection of women's rights in the workplace and energetic measures against violence against women. . . ."[21]

This is what the text of President Clinton's government program promises, in the paragraph entitled Strategy for Change. This proposition is a consequence of the fact that in the United States, domestic violence against women constitutes the most common crime, according to U.S. Attorney General Janet Reno, as reported by Notimex.[22]

Speaking in Dade County, Florida, Reno confirmed that 40% of the infractions committed were linked to the abuse of women in a family context.[23]

"On January 31, [1994], *USA-Today* reported that 12.5 million U.S. women aged over 12 are victims of violent assault every year."[24]

In mid-1993, the National Association of Women Executives published a study demonstrating that women have found it impossible to break through the sex barrier that excludes them from better jobs and decision-making.

According to the study, U.S. women also earn as much as 25% less than men in some sectors of production.

21. Luis Báez Delgado. "Carta pública a un presidente" (Open Letter to a President), in *Granma* daily, June 2, 1994, 5. (Retranslated from Spanish.)
22. Nicanor León Cotayo. "La mujer en Estados Unidos" (Women in the United States), in *Trabajadores* newspaper, July 18, 1994, 6.
23. Ibid.
24. Notimex. Miami, January 31, 1994.

The Association's report adds that only 2.6% of responsible positions within the upper ranks of 500 U.S. companies are occupied by women, while, in spite of having seven million more votes than men, as a gender they comprise 6% of the House of Representatives and 11% of the Senate.

In addition, there are no women in 23 of the 50 state legislatures in the Union and 46 of the country's 50 governor's offices are filled by men.[25]

On the other hand, the Cuban system offers women significant guarantees. Article 44 of the Constitution states:

Women and men have the same rights in the economic, political, cultural and social fields, as well as in the family.

The state guarantees women the same opportunities and possibilities as men, in order to achieve women's full participation in the development of the country.

The state organizes such institutions as children's daycare centers, semiboarding schools and boarding schools, homes for the elderly and services to make it easier for the working family to carry out its responsibilities.

The state looks after women's health as well as that of their offspring, giving working women paid maternity leave before and after giving birth and temporary work options compatible with their maternal activities.

The state strives to create all the conditions which help make real the principle of equality.[26]

25. Nicanor León Cotayo. Op. cit., 6.
26. *Constitution of the Republic of Cuba,* loc. cit.

This demonstrates the difference between Cuba and a highly developed country like Switzerland, where, for example, there are no school cafeterias, making it necessary for 60% of women to find temporary jobs, also the lowest paid.[27]

A glance at the statistics is enough to give some idea of the decisive role—thanks to the equal rights enjoyed by women in Cuba—that this significant sector of society has played, is playing and will continue to play in the construction of a more equitable and just world, in spite of the setbacks resulting from the special period. The latter, given women's dual function as workers and housewifes, has placed a greater burden of responsibility on their shoulders.

27. Juana Carrasco Martín. Op. cit., 48.

Table 6
Women's Participation in Main Economic Sectors

Sector	Women (%)	Women technicians (%)	Women in administrative positions (%)
Health	72.0	79.9	35.8
Education	69.0	70.2	48.6
Tourism	44.0	52.0	25.0
Science and technology	43.0	41.7	26.1
Agriculture	26.5	32.6	11.6
Total	50.9	55.2	29.4

SOURCE: Compiled by the author from data taken from *Main Report to the 6th Congress of the Federation of Cuban Women,* Havana, 1995, 6-10.

Cuba is fighting to resist the impact of the economic blockade, to continue its development and to conserve its achievements. Women have had a great deal of responsibility in this undertaking, as the statistics show:

- Over half of them, 50.9%, work in the country's priority sectors.

- Over half of that work force, 52.2%, is fully qualified.

- Over a quarter, 29.4%, hold administrative positions.

- Over 40% of the total work force, 40.6%, is made up of women.

- Women comprise 59% of classroom teachers and 45% of the teaching staff in higher education.

- 42% of research positions are held by women.

- They comprise 43% of the total of workers in the scientific field, 53% at advanced levels.[28]

The following comparative table reveals how the special period has caused a decline in women's participation, brought about by an increased burden of domestic responsibilities resulting from the shortages.

Table 7

Women's Employment Structure According to Occupational Category

Occupational categories	1990	1994
Workers	19.5	20.9
Technicians	57.7	62.0
Administration	90.2	86.1
Services	62.6	60.3
Leaders	28.6	28.0

SOURCE: *Main Report to the 6th Congress...*, 12.

28. *Informe Central al VI Congreso de la Federación de Mujeres Cubanas* (Main Report to the 6th Congress of the Federation of Cuban Women), 1995, 12-14.

It is not hard to see that female employment in the service and administrative sectors and in leadership posts has suffered; however, society has not ignored vocational education and training for women, which increased by 7.1% during the same period.

These figures confirm that the Cuban system has understood that the participation of women, given that they constitute half of humanity, is essential for any nation's development.

There are 1107 day-care centers in the country, where 73% of children under six years of age are educated. Children in these centers receive quality care in order to ensure their pre-school training and to facilitate women's integration into the country's development process.

The Cuban social model consolidates, respects and defends the space gained by Cuban women. Within marriage, women have full rights that are extended to non-legalized or informal relationships. As a result, no discrimination is made—as occurs in other countries—between children born in and out of wedlock.

Comparing the Cuban social system with others, under which women are still waging bloody and bitter battles for equal opportunities in work, pay and, incredibly, for elemental rights such as suffrage and being able to decide when to have children, the distance still to be covered in our countries is apparent.

In Cuba, the retirement age for women is 55 years, five years less than that of men, with an option to continue working if they are able and willing to do so. Every retired person receives a pension for life.

Cuban women also have the right to take up arms to defend their nation. They have access to combat training and voluntary military service. The Federation of Cuban Women (FMC), likewise on a voluntary basis, groups together women aged 14 years and up and attends to all issues related to women in the social context.

A study by the International Labor Organization recently acknowledged that it will take women almost 500 years to gain equality with men in terms of holding positions of political and economic power. However, one of Cuba's visible achievements is that within the state power structures, female representation is 22.8%, while the global average of women parliamentarians stands at 10%, reaching 18% in Canada.[29]

29. Juana Carrasco Martín. Op.cit., 48.

HEALTH CARE

What justly belongs to the people cannot be given as charity.

—José Manuel Bárcenas, priest and professor at the Workers University of Gijón, Asturias

Hillary Clinton, speaking to Texan nurses on June 11, 1994, indignantly stated that she didn't want to hear one more story about children turned away from a hospital, or of a woman denied a biopsy on what could be a breast tumor.[30]

In the same speech, the first lady acknowledged that there are 40 million persons without medical insurance and several millions more underinsured in the United States.[31] Some sources quote a figure of 70 million citizens lacking health care services.

During the Bush administration, the health and education budget of the United States was reduced by 150 billion dollars.

An AFP news dispatch dated June 1993 reads:

> Bill Clinton's Democratic administration has come up with a million-dollar plan to combat the low immunization rate—another of the problems facing U.S. children—given that the country figures 17th in the international listings of children under one year vaccinated against polio, below even Pakistan. If the children are non-white, the rate plunges to 70th place, below Burundi, Nicaragua, Trinidad and Tobago, Mongolia and Viet Nam.[32]

In spite of this sad reality, what was the U.S. Senate's response to the president's plan?

---

30. Notimex. San Antonio, June 11, 1994.
31. Ibid.
32. Juana Carrasco Martín. Op. cit., 48.

> On Wednesday, the Republican minority triumphed in the U.S. Senate by employing a political delaying tactic that destroyed Bill Clinton's economic stimulation bill, Prensa Latina reports.
>
> By way of this 16.3 billion dollar plan, Clinton hoped to inject some strength into the ailing U.S. economy by creating jobs.
>
> Through spokesperson Dee Myers, Clinton stated that he felt disappointed and accused the Republicans of playing at politics. . . .
>
> The plan included funds for a children's vaccination campaign. . . .[33]

For its part, the IPS agency issued an alarming news dispatch from Geneva, dated June 21, 1994, covering a UNICEF report that claims:

> Two hundred and fifty million [children] lose their sight every year due to a lack of vitamin A...; 140,000, especially in the developing countries, are disabled as a result of poliomyelitis; one million die from measles; and over three million from pneumonia.[34]

Bernard Sanders, the only independent U.S. congressman, emphasized during his last reelection campaign for the state of Vermont that this scenario is not limited to the Third World.

> With every passing day, our economic development bears a closer resemblance to any of the so-called developing

---

33. "Revés en el senado para plan económico de Clinton" (Senate Setback for Clinton's Economic Plan), in *Granma* daily, April 23, 1993, 3.

34. "Opina congresista que EE.UU. está en camino de convertirse en oligarquía" (Congressman States U.S. Is On the Way to Becoming an Oligarchy), in *Granma* daily, July 30, 1994, 8.

or Third World countries, and 22% of our children (14 million) are living below the poverty line. Every day, five million children go hungry on the streets of the United States, while two million U.S. adults (many of them mentally ill) wander the streets because they have nowhere to live.[35]

The reality exposed by Mr. Sanders is but a part of the countless additional health disasters related to the acute poverty endured by many more people than those referred to by the independent senator.

A further Prensa Latina news dispatch from Quito, dated August 31, 1994 says:

Two-thirds of the infant population of Asia, Africa and Latin America and the Caribbean are victims of malnutrition, and one million die every year, according to the United Nations Children's Fund (UNICEF).

[It adds] that over 45 million children under six are currently suffering from acute poverty. It notes that over one and a half million children up to 14 years of age die every year as a consequence of that poverty, mainly expressed in low nutrition and health indices.[36]

There are no health care guarantees for citizens in the U.S. Constitution or in those of many other nations. However, the Cuban Constitution states:

Everyone has the right to health protection and care. The state guarantees this right:

35. Ibid.
36. "Un millón de niños muere anualmente" (One Million Children Die Every Year), in *Granma* daily, September 1, 1994, 1.

-by providing free medical and hospital care by means of the installations of the rural medical service network, polyclinics, hospitals, preventative and specialized treatment centers;

- by providing free dental care;

- by promoting the health publicity campaigns, health education, regular medical examinations, general vaccinations and other measures to prevent the outbreak of disease. All the population cooperates in these activities and plans through the social and mass organizations.[37]

Within the Cuban system, infants receive medical attention from the first months after conception. If, out of carelessness or ignorance (highly exceptional cases), a pregnant woman fails to attend appointments, the health care infrastructure provides for medical staff to search out the mother-to-be and offer her professional care (check-ups, examinations, vitamins, all free of charge) until the birth of the child, who subsequently comes under the care of a pediatrician. Persuading and convincing every mother to breast feed is an aspect of preventative medicine that the country hasn't overlooked. The encouraging results have impressed representatives from the WHO, PAHO and UNICEF.

However, in 1992, Mrs. Clinton confessed to the continent's first ladies that in her country, 22% of pregnant women receive no prenatal care.[38]

Innovative techniques for the early detection of pathologies, applied en masse in Cuba, have reduced to a minimum the birth of infants with congenital or inherited deformities. The tiny minority of children born with some problem are given specialized medical care and generous resources to improve their standard and quality of life.

37. *Constitution of the Republic of Cuba,* loc. cit.
38. Ernesto Montero Acuña. "¿Cima or cisma?" (Peak or Pit?), in *Trabajadores* newspaper, December 12, 1994, 7.

News dispatches continue to be a good source of information and an irreplaceable instrument in terms of this investigation:

> Experts convened in Washington by the Pan American Health Organization (PAHO) praised the Cuban measles elimination program....

> The 11th technical advisory group meeting of the PAHO's extended immunization program, which discussed the subject of measles, also confirmed a decrease in this disease in Latin American countries, due to immunization campaigns for children aged 1-14 years, taken from the Cuban experience.[39]

U.S. medical scientist Dorothy Horstmann stated in a meeting in Havana on June 8, 1994, that Cubans have undeniably carried out successful work in a very efficient way. She added that poliomyelitis has not only been eradicated, but that the virus itself is not in circulation in the country.

Dr. Ciro de Cuadros, coordinator of the PAHO's immunization program and special vaccine advisor to the WHO directorate, referred to the Cuban government's political will in terms of the immunization program's continuity as a significant contribution to the elimination of polio in Cuba, and called the granting to the country of a Poliomyelitis Eradication Certificate as a historic moment. Moreover, he affirmed that the Cuban practice of "immunization through campaigning", with the active participation of mass organizations, was a model for the rest of the world. He added that he had learned two important lessons in Cuba: political will and popular participation directed towards these ends.

The international commission responsible for presenting Poliomyelitis Eradication Certificates was established by the PAHO as an independent body made up of experts and highly respected scientific figures.

39. José A. de la Osa. "14 meses sin sarampión" (14 Months Without Measles), in *Granma* daily, September 15, 1994, 1.

Dr. George Alleyne, deputy director of the PAHO, stated on a recent visit to Cuba that he was very impressed with the efforts Cuba was making to preserve people's health in the midst of so many economic difficulties. He affirmed that the island's social indices and development programs are "the envy of the world; Cuba has worked wonders."[40]

These aforementioned organizations confirm, endorse and praise the system and infrastructure created by Cuba to immunize its infant population against twelve diseases. (See Table 9 at the end of the chapter.)

In 1993 there were only two recorded cases of tetanus, two of measles, two of German measles, 11 of mumps and 11 of whooping cough in the country, meaning that they can be considered to be virtually eliminated.

A further useful news item for comparative purposes:

> According to the WHO, no less than three million persons die of tuberculosis throughout the world every year, the majority in developing countries, while four to five million contagious cases are reported.

> In New York City the figures rose from 1,517 cases in 1980 to 3,520 in 1990.[41]

The tuberculosis figures for New York translate into approximately 20 cases for every 100,000 inhabitants. In the city of Havana, over the same period, the figures fell from 395 to 171 cases, or 8.5 for every 100,000 inhabitants.

Early detection of this disease in Cuba by way of appropriate mechanisms and structures expedites prompt cure. While undergoing treatment, sufferers receive a special diet and 100%

40. "Cuba es un ejemplo en materia social" (Cuba is an Example in the Social Context), in *Granma* daily, June 16, 1994, 8.
41. Bárbara Avendaño Pérez. "La tuberculosis no admite perder tiempo" (Tuberculosis Can't Wait), in *Tribuna* newspaper, July 17, 1994, 7.

of their wages. Treatment is free and can be given in the patient's own home under the control of the family doctor and nurse system—a marvelous institution created by Cubans to respond to the population's primary health care needs, by providing a doctor and nurse for approximately every 140 families, and based in each neighborhood in a specially built home-office or in already existing consultation facilities.

To guarantee efficient medical and hospital service to all citizens, Cuba has approximately 55,000 doctors (one for every 200 inhabitants, the highest per capita in the world), 72,700 nurses (many of them university trained), 308,800 health workers, 65,600 beds in 277 hospitals, 83 intensive therapy wards and a health care budget of over one billion pesos for the year 1994.[42]

In this way, Cuba provides a powerful health care system working on behalf of all the people, who have free access to medical check-ups and examinations; vaccines; kidney, cornea, bone-marrow and heart transplants; lithotripsy or gallstone operations; computerized axial tomography; treatment for vitiligo, obesity, heart disease, psoriasis, pigmentary retinosis and sexual dysfunctions; interferon treatment for cancer, chemotherapy, cosmetic surgery, ophthalmic microsurgery, prosthesis implants and many other services that would make this list interminable. All these are also available to foreign citizens wishing to receive treatment in Cuba at competitive prices through the health tourism option.

The effectiveness and quality of the Cuban medical system lies in the fact that public health care is no longer a market commodity. In Cuba, doctors are not businesspeople, and in order to fully understand these achievements, one has to grasp

42. "Inaugurado Biotecnología '94" (Biotechnology '94 Inaugurated), in *Granma* daily, November 29, 1994, 1, and Miguel A. Gainza. "¿Le da vergüenza, Presidente?" (Aren't You Ashamed, Mr. President?), in *Sierra Maestra* newspaper, August 6, 1994, 6.

the material and spiritual changes in a society where doctors, divested of mercantilism, identify with a community all the more generous for being free of the petty selfishness that corrodes societies divided into antagonistic social classes. When their basic needs are covered, people regain their humanity. That is why the situations that prompted Hillary Clinton's painful words to Texan nurses cannot arise in Cuba.

Many Latin American government programs, and even the Democratic U.S. president's program entitled "People Come First", include nobly constructed plans that are never materialized and remain as frustrated wishes or deliberately false promises. In terms of the Cuban model, the constant exercise of a sensibility and political will protagonized by the masses themselves not only guarantees that the Constitution is fulfilled, but that it is steadily improved. It's like a sociopolitical system designed by poets who perceive democracy as a profound love for human beings. However, this love is reflected in concrete figures, such as an infant mortality rate of 9.5 per 1,000 live births (1994), a life expectancy of 75.7 years (1990-1995) and preventive medicine on a mass scale.[43]

This qualitative jump is founded on an intelligently devised program that includes, among other services, HIV screening of the entire population, regular Pap tests, periodic general check-ups, regular mammographies, strategies for prenatal risk cases (women with diabetes or hypertension, smokers, undernourished or underweight women, and those with a family history of genetic defects), widescale dental and psychological care, treatment from early infancy, even dolphin therapy.[44]

A curious piece of information worth noting is that immediately after Fidel Castro came to power in 1959, Washington unleashed a campaign—one of many—that provoked the exo-

---

43. René Márquez Castro. Op. cit., 10, and *World Almanac 1994,* 137.
44. Orfilio Peláez. "Uso de delfines en tratamientos para niños" (Dolphin Therapy for Children), in *Granma* daily, August 27, 1994, 3.

dus of 3,000 of the island's 6,000 doctors. Then one year after President Kennedy's assassination, the U.S. government prohibited the export of medicines to Cuba and pressured other countries to do the same. As a result, the Cuban social regime came into existence in a situation similar to that in Guatemala and Bolivia today—to give just two examples—with over 2,000 persons per doctor—according to the *World Almanac*—and without medicines. Which could be described as starting almost from zero.

We all know what psychiatric hospitals in the Third World are like, no different from Havana's Mazorra Hospital, as it was called up until 1959. Today this center is one of the finest examples of what a human being can strive for. Thousands of visitors are aware of this hospital's achievements and of its contributions to medical science throughout the world.

Recently President Clinton succeeded in legalizing abortion in the United States. Women in the United States have obtained by legislation what Cuban women have held for over 30 years: the right to decide when to have children.

In Cuba, fitting intra-uterine contraceptive devices or carrying out vasectomies—both free of charge—are routine procedures. Together with contraceptive pills and condoms, these are the most commonly recommended methods of preventing an unplanned pregnancy, and thus the possibility of resorting to abortion. An organized sex education campaign completes the conditions for the provision of this supremely important right, one that's taken for granted: the right to come into the world as a wanted child. This minimizes traumatized mothers and child victims, and allows children to grow up with sufficient love and the necessary psycho-emotional equilibrium.

The result is voluntary birth control decided upon by a couple with no outside pressure. The mature decision of free and educated persons to procreate presupposes their increased happiness, and leads to a more conscientious attitude in this regard.

One could add that democracy is also about increased independence and therefore, more freedom. It's not difficult to imagine the freedom and enormous security those gains give couples, and especially women.

The Cuban socioeconomic system goes further than insuring that newborns come into the world as wanted children, that they are healthy and loved, and that they learn to read and write; these children continue to be cared for and enjoy many other rights central to their integral development.

Table 8
Cuban Vaccination Program Covering
100% of Child Population
(This vaccination rate ranks Cuba among the first places in the world)

	New born	1 month	3 months	4 months	5 months	5½ months	6 months	1 year
B.C.G.	V							
H.B.V.	V	R					R	
D.P.T.			V	R	R			R
Meningitis B and C			V			R		
P.R.S.								V
D.T.								
A.T.								
Tetanus								
Polio		V						

	2 years, 11 months, 29 days old	6 years old	10 years old (in 5th grade)	11 years, 11 months, 29 days old	13 years old (in 8th grade)	14 years old (in 9th grade)	16 years old (in 11th grade)
D.T.		V					
A.T.			V		R		R
Tetanus						V	
Polio	R		R	R			

SOURCE: Compiled by the author from data taken from Cuban Public Health Ministry Sources.

Legend:
V.........Vaccination
R.........Reactivation
B.C.G.....Anti-tuberculosis
H.B.V.....Hepatitis B

D.P.T......Diphtheria-whooping cough-tetanus
P.R.S......Mumps-German measles-measles
D.T......Diphtheria-tetanus
A.T......Anti-typhus

Table 9

Population, Infant Mortality Rate and Average Number of Inhabitants Per Doctor (the Americas)

Country	Population	Infant mortality (per 1000 live births)	Number of inhabitants per doctor*
Argentina	32, 60, 680	28.8	600
Bolivia	6, 344, 300	84.8	1, 062
Brazil	153, 322, 000	57.0	685
Chile	13, 386, 000	16.9	2, 930
Colombia	33, 613, 000	37.0	1, 079
Costa Rica	3, 064, 000	13.7	1, 129
Cuba	10, 736, 000	14.2	207
Dominican Rep.	7, 313, 000	56.5	934
Ecuador	10, 851, 000	57.4	826
El Salvador	5, 376, 000	45.6	1, 603
Guatemala	10, 029, 414	48.5	2, 238

Haiti	6, 625, 000	95.0	6, 087
Honduras	5, 265, 000	59.7	1, 695
Mexico	87, 836, 000	35.2	600
Nicaragua	3, 999, 000	52.1	1, 678
Panama	2, 466, 000	20.8	840
Paraguay	4, 397, 000	47.0	1, 593
Peru	22, 914, 606	75.8	1, 000
Puerto Rico	3, 551, 000	17.0	350
United States	252, 688, 000	9.0**	404
Uruguay	3, 112, 000	20.0	344
Venezuela	20, 266, 000	33.2	595

SOURCE: Compiled by the author from data taken from "¿Le da vergüenza, Presidente?" (Aren't You Ashamed, Mr. President?), by Miguel A. Gainza, *Sierra Maestra* newspaper, Santiago de Cuba, August 6, 1994. "¿Para quién?" (For Whom?), by Ernesto Montero Acuña, *Trabajadores* newspaper, Havana, October 31, 1994. "Inaugurado Biotecnología '94" (Biotechnology '94 Inaugurated), *Granma* daily, Havana, November 29, 1994. World Almanac 1994, loc. cit.

* These statistics are from 1990-1995, except for Puerto Rico (1988), and Bolivia and Brazil (1990).

** It is said that in Washington, D.C. there are 30 deaths per 1,000 live births, in Harlem 25 per 1,000, and in New York 10.2 per 1,000.

SCIENCE AND TECHNOLOGY

After a serious and detailed study, there can be no doubt that humanity's scientific heritage has also been enriched by Cuba's valiant contributions, despite the relentless efforts of the United States to destroy its Revolution with measures that have outlasted all records in contemporary history.

It comes as a real shock to most visitors to find a Cuba totally different from what is depicted by the powerful mass media, oriented and manipulated to a major degree by the United States.

Here is a small Third World country—in addition to its significant gains in the field of social development, exceeding those of the developed nations in some sectors—using and creating advanced technologies that can compete with the best in the world. This provokes more than admiration because an observer cannot understand this paradox: on the one hand, Cuba has been coming up with solutions to weighty and serious problems facing the underdeveloped countries; and on the other, it has had to contend with the U.S.-imposed economic blockade for 35 years, so how has it managed to reach those levels?

In today's dynamic world, it is impossible to achieve any development without creating the essential scientific bases on which to use and create cutting-edge technology. This has been fully grasped by the leaders of the Cuban system and incorporated as an absolute truth by the people.

The following UNESCO table shows the number of scientists in some countries of the developed world and in other regions:

Table 10
Percentage of Scientists and Engineers
(per 1,000 inhabitants)

Country	Scientists and engineers
Japan	4.7
United States	3.8
Former USSR	3.3
EEC	2.2
Latin America and the Third World	between 0.5 and 0.9

SOURCE: Compiled by the author from data taken from "Retos que enfrentamos" (The Challenges We Face), by Rosa Elena Simeón Negrín, in *Bohemia* magazine, Havana, November 11, 1994, 21-22.

These are the rates attained by capitalist countries after 400 years of this system's existence. However, Cuba—after just 36 years of Revolution—shows a ratio of 1.6 scientists and engineers per every 1,000 inhabitants, in spite of deliberate attempts to sabotage this undertaking. These statistics place Cuba at the head of the Third World. Cuba's scientific potential, according to the Cuban science and technology minister, includes over 10,000 professionals in the field of scientific research, along with over 17,000 highly qualified professors who, as part of their teaching activity, undertake research in 49 university faculties and 210 research centers. In addition, the country has 14 scientific complexes linked to 280 production and 78 research centers, staffed by some 33,000 men and women with different levels of specialization.[45]

This explains the confusion of visitors to Cuba on finding themselves in a Third World country which has managed to insert itself into the competitive and, up until very recently, exclusive world of the international pharmaceuticals market, controlled by the transnationals. Academic advances in the spheres of genetic engineering and biotechnology and the creation of Cuban-made technologies have produced prodigious successes.

The meningococcus type BC vaccine (VA-MENGOC-BC), the only one of its kind in the world, was developed by Cuban scientists. Every day the list of countries immunizing their infant populations with this vaccine grows longer. The economic blockade prohibits this important product being marketed in the United States, due to its Cuban origin. The children of the citizens of the "most democratic" country in the world cannot be immunized like Cuban, Brazilian, Colombian, Argentine and other infants. There should be some mechanism through which a parent whose child falls victim to meningitis in the

45. Rosa Elena Simeón Negrín, minister of science, technology and the environment. "Retos que enfrentamos" (The Challenges We Face), in *Bohemia* magazine, November 11, 1994, 21-22.

United States can file suit against the U.S. government for failing to prevent this terrible disease.

The vaccine against hepatitis B, also created by Cuban scientists, is a further contribution to humanity's well-being.

Then comes PPG or Ateromisol, a natural medicine which reduces cholesterol levels. Considered as highly advantageous because it doesn't attack positive fats, this drug also provides the beneficial secondary effect of increasing blood circulation.

Cuban laboratories have also developed Melagenina, an extract of the human placenta stimulating melanine production and used in the treatment of vitiligo, an ailment that affects millions of people around the world.

Other important medications developed by Cuban scientists are the epidermal growth factor, which contributes to the rapid regeneration of skin tissue, very effective in the treatment of burns, and streptokinase, a drug used to prevent miocardiac strokes, which was discovered by two U.S. scientists some years ago, but at a prohibitive cost. It is being produced for the first time in Cuba using recombinant methods.

Using similar methods, Cuba has also obtained the Interleucina-2 (IL-2) protein, a biological response modifier, capable of increasing immune response to neoplastic tumors. This medical product is marketed by just two transnationals asking 900 dollars per milligram of injectable biologically active protein.

Cuba's work in the sphere of monoclonal antibodies is extensive. The country has won considerable international prestige in this field.

Medical equipment produced by national technology has given Cuba an exclusive foothold in international markets with innovations such as the Neurónica,[46] Medicid,[47] Suma,[48] and

46. Neurónica. Cuban device for the detection of hearing problems in the first months of life.
47. Medicid 3E. Computerized system used to carry out electroencephalograms, neurophysiological studies, cerebral scanning, integral evaluation of the function of the central nervous system.
48. Suma. Cuban laboratory device used in the diagnosis of congenital diseases and others of infectious origin, such as AIDS and hepatitis.

Diramic.[49] Other non-exclusive nationally manufactured products such as magnetic resonance tomographs, radioactive isotopes and complex prostheses, also assume technological expertise, and give Cuba a respected position in the Third World on a par with the most developed countries in some important sectors. Cuba also produces interferon and other drugs used in the treatment of cancer and other diseases, and which are available in only a few of the developed countries.

This small island is well endowed with its own unique therapies and surgical techniques. Up until now, it is the only country in the world to treat persons suffering from pigmentary retinosis with an effective surgical technique preventing the progress of the disease, pioneered by Cuban scientist Orfilio Peláez. This medical advance gained Peláez the Vision Prize, awarded in Beverley Hills, California, by the International Retinitis Pigmentosa Association to persons who have given 20 years of service to combating blindness and have made a significant contribution to ophthalmology.

Cuban orthopedic specialists have revolutionized the treatment of bone traumatology with significant contributions. Professor Rodrigo Álvarez Cambras' external fixators introduced a substantially new and innovative technique and are in wide demand on the international market. Álvarez Cambras' innovative hip surgery techniques have also made a successful contribution to medicine.

"Using the white coral that grows in abundance on the insular platform, Cuba is producing a new type of biomaterial produced only in France and the United States. This biomaterial can be used as a substitute for bone fragments lost due to accidents or tumors."[50]

49. Diramic. Laboratory equipment, also Cuban developed, for conducting rapid antibiograms to determine the appropriate antibiotic for the patient.
50. Pedro Juan Gutiérrez. "Biomateriales. Huesos en coral" (Biomaterials, Bones Made of Coral), in *Bohemia* magazine, June 25, 1993, p. 38.

The International Neurological Restoration Center, located in Cuba, has similar prestige. The refined surgical technique of implanting embryonic tissue in the human brain to eliminate Parkinson's disease has elevated Cuban medical science to lofty new heights. The August 14, 1992 issue of the *Science* journal states that the injection of fetal tissue into both cerebral hemispheres in just one operation (stereotaxic neuro-restoration) is unique to Cuba. According to the journal, the Cuban institution has achieved the highest success rates in the world with this operation, far exceeding the United States, Sweden and Great Britain.[51]

In the field of veterinary genetics, the world is indebted to Cuba for the creation of a new breed of quality cattle, productive in tropical conditions and obtained through the scientifically controlled crossing of the zebu, a tropical cattle highly resistant to disease and high temperatures but a low producer, with the Holstein, a good producer but with little resistance to disease and tropical temperatures. One of these animals broke the international milk yield record with 125 liters of milk in one day over three milkings. The average milk production for this breed is two or three liters short of the highest averages in the world, held by Israel.

Currently, the heavy use of chemical products, fertilizers, pesticides and herbicides has led to global concern over the destruction of the biosphere. During the last 15 years, Cuba has put a great deal of effort into developing biological products as a replacement for chemicals, with some promising results. These scientific contributions could be of international benefit, since their application could be adopted in other countries of the world. On two occasions, reputable U.S. scientists have praised Cuban advances in this area, a field in which those visitors confirmed that the United States lags 15 years behind.

51. José A. de la Osa. "Ficción hecha realidad" (Fiction Come True), in *Granma* daily, February 13, 1993, 10-11.

In the meantime, Cuban scientific methodology and organization has resulted in its own contribution: scientific complexes located throughout the country with regular information exchanges, thus maximizing possibilities of finding solutions to various problems that arise. In Cuba, the image of the isolated scientist working on the margins doesn't exist.

Cuba's scientific advances have not come about by chance, they are based on a sound infrastructure of organized efforts requiring financial input and the systematic training of qualified personnel capable of meeting the challenges that contemporary realities impose on a Third World country. A complete list of Cuban contributions would not only be extremely long, it would also soon be out of date; the country is continuing work on ambitious projects and the results can be seen on a daily basis: vaccines for humans and animals, diverse types of medical products, innovative therapies, etc.

The economic blockade also impedes the international availability of many of those products by hindering their entry into the world market. In Cuba, prices are competitive and products are of high quality.

As a consequence of the economic blockade, spare parts are hard to come by. Some years ago, this gave rise to an original movement of innovators who took it upon themselves to find solutions to the many concrete problems regularly arising in various spheres of production and services. This movement has continued to develop and has produced a new phenomenon, unmatched in any other country. At the last science and technology forum in Havana, 263,000 authors presented 256,000 solutions in their papers and seminars presented to more than one million participants. An awareness of a powerful driving force and the unbreakable will of people who understand that intelligence is one of their strongest weapons is clearly visible in this unparalleled movement.

This kind of scientific-technological event and others held on a regular basis by the sector's trade union all contribute to the constant enrichment of the country's scientific store.

SCHOOL OF LOVE

Love does not give more than itself and does not take more
than itself.
—Khalil Gibran, *The Prophet*

From my Third World researcher's vision it's difficult to remain neutral—in relation to the economic blockade—faced with a society that constantly demonstrates values long disappeared in other countries. Such values have to be characteristic of any society calling itself democratic. That is why it's impossible to remain neutral after witnessing the injustice of a genocidal economic blockade that indiscriminately affects all members of Cuban society.

It's impossible to stay on the margins if one compares Cuban society with the conditions facing our Latin American peoples, or when recalling that two million violent crimes, resulting in a total of 26,250 recorded deaths, took place in the United States in 1994. This violence is reflected in all that country's mass media, particularly in television and film, and this serves to justify hatred, individualism, misanthropy and ferocious selfishness.

This inhumane school that degrades and tramples over human beings is counterposed by Cuban philanthropy and altruism, a school of love that extols and dignifies people, giving them their genuine human dimensions. Values such as comradeliness, internationalism, solidarity, patriotism and integrity are the backbone of the principles defended by the Cuban model.

The Cuban people's virtues are thrown into relief by viewing evidence like Estela Bravo's documentary on the so-called "excludables" in the United States. Her film shows Cubans incarcerated for years in that country, with no legal justification for their imprisonment and no legal protection; they are victims, moreover, of torture, mistreatment and deliberate drugging so that they can be categorized as mentally ill, which entitles the prison to a larger budget. Estela Bravo's documentary also reveals the powerlessness of their families—from whom they were sometimes forcibly separated—contradictions at official level, and the most flagrant violations of the human rights of the thousands of people caught in this situation.

Cuba is facing a real war, albeit without bombs. Nevertheless, panic is not rife, and discipline and organization have been maintained. Measures adopted to cushion the economic blockade's effects are always designed to have a minimal effect on the population. The people remain confident that the nation will recover from the crisis of the *special period in peacetime*.

The willingness of parents to sacrifice their lives for their children is not unheard of; but in today's world, the sentiment of solidarity that leads people to give up their lives for another human being in the name of concepts like dignity, justice, freedom, equality, honor and independence is practically unknown.

Today's Cubans have a new concept of life, the result of an education that takes the best from distinct philosophies and cultures. This has enabled them to resist the merciless war waged on them for decades by a powerful and unscrupulous enemy. And they have managed to resist without losing their sensitivity, generosity and serenity in the face of provocations and hostile actions that have taken away their loved ones. Nor have they allowed themselves to be dragged down by selfishness in the face of shortages, or get caught up in hate. On the contrary, they are standing up to the difficulties while keeping the banners of love, respect and human solidarity flying. People in Cuba advocate simplicity and modesty and an unyielding fight against injustice and inequality. This unswerving resistance is proof of an exceptional phenomenon that deserves deeper analysis and close attention to its development. It is a sad fact that some governments, faced with such an uncommon and original social system, choose to assume an ostrich response, when they could learn a lot from it.

In Cuba one simply needs to inform the population that 100,000 or 500,000 blood donations are needed in order to obtain its immediate cooperation. Many people in the world who have fallen victim to major natural disasters have experienced this generosity. The country's blood derivatives industry is flourishing on those donations.

Almost all Cubans are voluntary organ donors, an unusual feature in capitalist countries. This is the result of an education which encourages a sense of selflessness. Cubans welcome the opportunity to be of use after their death by freely donating vital organs to save or improve the life of another person. Such wishes are expressed during their lives and reflected in their personal identity documents. Nevertheless, doctors do not make any decisions in relation to a deceased donor's organs until they have obtained the consent of family members.

At the same time, a great many Cubans have also donated their labor in 55 countries of the world.

Over 10,000 children and hundreds of adults, victims of the Chernobyl nuclear plant tragedy, have received free specialized medical treatment in Cuba, given to them with much love, even after Ukraine ceased to be a socialist country.

Recently, Cuba also offered to make its therapeutic surgical technique for the treatment of pigmentary retinosis freely available throughout the world, since not everyone suffering from this disease can travel to the island for treatment.

In addition, 26,000 Cuban teachers and professors have taken their educational skills to a great many Third World countries, once again on a voluntary basis and free of charge. Over 25,000 foreign students from every continent have been awarded scholarships by the Cuban authorities to study in the island's universities.

Schools, hospitals, homes and even a sugar mill have been constructed by Cuban workers and donated to countries with greater needs, in spite of the difficult conditions imposed by the economic blockade, which has caused losses estimated at 45 billion dollars over more than 30 years.

The total number of refugees from various countries who have received housing and financial help in Cuba while adjusting to their new conditions runs into the thousands. Chileans, Argentines, Uruguayans, Venezuelans, Colombians, Panamanians, Nicaraguans, Salvadorans, Guatemalans, Dominicans, Africans, and Palestinians and other nationals have fled to this Caribbean island from regimes where they faced persecution for wanting a more equitable life for their peoples. In Cuba, they have found the human warmth they needed to recover from physical wounds and alleviate spiritual ones.

Without a doubt, one of the most beautiful demonstrations of altruism and internationalism is Cuba's voluntary and selfless cooperation in African liberation struggles, particularly in Angola. Cuba's assistance contributed to Namibia's independence, as well as to the process in South Africa that culminated in the defeat of that most inhuman, oppressive and humiliating of all regimes: apartheid.

It would be a lengthy exercise to recount all the factors confirming that in one sense, the U.S. government is right: that the democratic model proposed by the United States doesn't exist in Cuba. Rather, the system that does exist could well be called a model or school of love. In Denmark, the organizing committee for the Development Summit, sponsored by the United Nations Industrial Development Organization (UNIDO), referred to the Cuban regime as a model of development to be imitated, and to Cuba's presence at the meeting as essential.

PART TWO

GENESIS AND DEVELOPMENT OF A CONFLICT

Independence is one thing, and revolution another. Independence in the United States arrived with Washington; and the revolution with Lincoln.

—José Martí

Right from January 1959, the United States initiated a fierce battle against the newly emerged independent state, making massive efforts to suppress the youthful and daring process underway. It also mounted—internally as well as externally—a series of actions aimed at frustrating the Cuban rebels' aspirations of independence, sovereignty and freedom.

In reality, this battle did not begin in 1959. It is derived from a claim stated by Washington long, long ago, the origins of which date back to 1807, when Thomas Jefferson, third president of the Union, declared that he had always viewed Cuba as the most important addition to the U.S. state system.

Such aspirations were preceded by concrete events that confirmed the nascent power's expansionist intentions. In 1803, the United States had bought the state of Louisiana from Napoleon, and later, in 1819, it acquired the state of Florida from Spain.

In 1823, U.S. President James Monroe designed his famous doctrine of "America for the Americans". Other theories and doctrines clearly revealing annexationist intentions appeared, such as the "Manifest Destiny" and the "ripe fruit" theories, alluding to the inevitability of Cuba falling into U.S. hands once separated from Spain. In 1845, Texas was annexed, and in 1848, Mexico was stripped of half its territory.

At the same time, the United States offered Spain a price for the island of Cuba in a formal sales proposition. As a result of this policy, two basic tendencies appeared in Cuba: a minority group, encouraged by the United States, advocating annexation—the so-called annexationists—and the independence advocates' majority, determined to prevent this from happening.

In 1898, the 20th president, McKinley, partially achieved that long-held American dream. After the defeat of the Spanish armies by Cuban patriots—in a long and bloody battle lasting thirty years—the United States blew up the *Maine*, one of its own war ships, in the bay of Havana, on a night when there just happened to be no officers on board, only the ship's crew, most of whom were black. On the pretext of that "aggression", attributed of course to Spain, the United States occupied Puerto Rico, the Philippines and—finally—took control in Cuba.

The Cubans never forgave the United States for frustrating their independence and castrating their sovereignty through an amendment imposed on their Constitution during the island's military occupation. And, as if that weren't enough, a piece of Cuban territory was amputated so as to install a U.S. naval base on it.

The fact that Fidel Castro rescued Cuba's national sovereignty and dignity, thus vindicating the struggle of those who fought before him and dispatching a century and a half of U.S. expansionist, annexationist and hegemonic aspirations—or the dream of converting Cuba, like Puerto Rico, into a colony—is really the central motive for the inflamed hatred that successive U.S. administrations have shown towards Cuba. The other arguments wielded to maintain, increase and justify their aggressions against Martí's nation are no more than attempts to conceal the real root of the problem.

In one of his last letters, written a few days before his death in combat, José Martí wrote:

> I am in daily danger of giving my life for my country and duty, for I understand that duty and have the courage to

carry it out—the duty of preventing the United States from spreading through the Antilles as Cuba gains its independence, and from overpowering with that additional strength our lands of America. All I have done so far, and all I will do, is for this purpose.[52]

Further on he notes:

I am doing my duty here. The Cuban war, a reality of higherpriority than the vague and scattered desires of the Cubanand Spanish annexationists, whose alliance with the Spanish government would only give them relative power, has come to America in time to prevent Cuba's annexation to the United States, even against all those freely used forces. The United States will never accept from a country at war, nor can it incur, the hateful and absurd commitment of discouraging, on its account and with its weapons, an American war of independence, for the war will not accept annexation.[53]

The historical-political legacy contained in this document complements the ideas of Bolívar, who convened the Panama Congress without a U.S. presence and made his own contribution to the strengthening of Latin American roots and identity, and the independentist thinking of the La Demajagua patriots.[54] It also demonstrates that the defense of sovereignty and independence, and subsequent Cuban battles to attain, defend and preserve that independence, is not a recent concept.

Several generations of Cubans have been educated in those principles and, in their struggles, have forged a strong identity that distinguishes them as unswerving patriots. Those are the

52. José Martí. Quoted from Philip S. Forner. *Our America* (New York-London: Monthly Review Press, 1977), 439.

53. Ibid, 441.

54. Sugar mill in eastern Cuba, site of the first armed uprising for Cuban independence from Spanish colonial domination, on October 10, 1868.

profound values that U.S. propaganda attempts to demolish through its constant anti-Cuba barrage.

The apparent mystery of the "Cuba case" is that its political direction is in no way makeshift. It concerns human beings identified with their history and their people, they are the flesh and blood of a process of struggle with profound historical roots and great popular support. Its enemies are unaware of or underestimate this highly important aspect and that is the key to their continual errors.

There is nothing like history to help us to better understand the conflict. The March 16, 1889 issue of the U.S. newspaper *The Manufacturer* expressed the United States' latent intentions in an article entitled "Do We Want Cuba?". It states:

> The Cubans are not much more desirable. Added to the defects of the paternal race are effeminacy and an aversion to all effort, truly to the extent of illness. They are helpless, lazy, deficient in morals, and incapable by nature and experience of fulfilling the obligations of citizenship in a great and free republic.[55]

José Martí responded to the *Manufacturer* article with dignity and gallantry, exposing the writer's total ignorance of the character, the fighting history and the bravery of a hard-working and intelligent people who have stood out in almost all spheres of human activity.[56]

In 1898, U.S. Secretary of War J.G. Breckenbridge, issued instructions to General Nelson A. Miles on how to effect the annexation of Cuba and Puerto Rico.

> Cuba, with a larger territory, has a bigger population than Puerto Rico. This is composed of whites and blacks and Asians and mixes of these. The inhabitants are generally

55. José Martí, Op. cit., 228.
56. Ibid.

indolent and apathetic. It is obvious that the immediate annexation of these elements into our own federation would be madness and, before doing so, we must clean up the country, even if that requires using the same methods as those applied by divine providence in Sodom and Gomorrah; we must destroy everything within our cannons' radius of action, we must concentrate the blockade, so that hunger and its eternal companion, the plague, will undermine the civilian population and decimate the Cuban army.[57]

At that time, Adolf Hitler was barely nine years old. Those racist viewpoints, that arrogant attitude, that inhuman vision of the world and that manner of underestimating other peoples have molded a psychology that reflects negatively in the relationship between our peoples. In addition, any mutual understanding is made difficult by such fatuity and ignorance on the part of figures at decision-making level in the higher political echelons of the United States.

Contemporary generations of Cubans perceive their struggle for independence as one continuing fight, from La Demajagua up until now. Those who claim that the conflict between the United States and Cuba is the result of supposed violations of human rights in the latter country, or of legislation damaging to U.S. economic interests, are deliberately lying. The real origin of the conflict lies in the long-held hegemonic appetite of the United States. Cuba has always occupied a strategic position in that country's expansionist sights, set on the whole of our America.

57. Luis Báez Delgado. Op. cit., 4. (Retranslated from Spanish.)

THE ECONOMIC BLOCKADE, A WAR WITHOUT BOMBS

The United States seems to be predestined by Providence to plague the peoples of America with hunger and poverty, in the name of liberty.

—Simón Bolívar

"On February 2, when then President John F. Kennedy issued Proclamation 3447, decreeing a total economic blockade, he did so with the express objective of starving the Cuban people and forcing the collapse of the Revolution."[58]

In practice, the economic blockade began on May 14, 1964, when the White House officially prohibited the sale of any U.S. food supplies to Cuba. According to the Cuban news agency Prensa Latina, on September 23, 1994, Beinusz Szmukler, president of the American Bar Association (ABA), spoke out against the U.S. economic blockade of Cuba, describing it as an aggression in the context of international law. The PL news dispatch continues:

> For over 30 years, the island of Cuba, where there are no disappeared, murdered or tortured persons, has been subjected to an economic blockade that has caused huge deprivations for its people and serious obstacles to its development.
>
> Addressing the 10th ABA Continental Conference, Szmukler said that only those with a failed memory could believe that the motives for the superpower's hostility toward the island is derived from its alleged restrictions of political and human rights.

58. Nidia Díaz. "Motivación económica con ropaje político" (Economic Motivations in Political Clothing), in *Granma* daily, September 6, 1994, 4.

The real reason, he added, is that in spite of its difficulties, Cuba sets an example in terms of a distribution
of national income that ensures health care, education,
culture, social security, basic nutrition, and sports and
recreation for its entire population.

Szmukler affirmed...that the Cuban people have the right
to decide on their political, economic and social regime
without external interference.[59]

It's hard to imagine what it signifies for a country with a
surface area of barely 100,000 square kilometers and less than
11 million inhabitants to hear its nearby superpower neighbor
assert through its president—after 35 years of a singularly cruel
economic, commercial and financial blockade—that:

The United States has done more than any other country
to try and put an end to Castro's government. We have
done it through the Cuban Democracy Act (Torricelli),
the embargo. We have worked hard, often almost alone,
to this end, and we will continue doing so by all the rea-
sonable means at our disposal.[60]

This is the intention of a nation 85 times greater in size and
with 242 million more citizens than Cuba, with a military
budget of 263.8 billion dollars, 130 times the hard currency
income received by its victim in one year.

This is an obvious abuse on the part of the United States.

The economic blockade, a low intensity war, a war without
bombs, a state of siege, a slow death by starvation; any of these
labels can fit this unilateral measure imposed on Cuba by the
United States. Its negative effects are causing severe spiritual
and material damage to the Cuban population. Trade, health,

59. "Condena presidente de juristas americanos bloqueo a Cuba" (President
of American Jurists Condemns Blockade of Cuba), in *Granma* daily,
September 2, 1994, 5.

60. AP. Washington, August 19, 1994. (Retranslated from Spanish.)

education and teaching, culture, sports, recreation, finance, transportation, communications, technology, science, energy, industrial and agricultural production are all affected. And of course, all this has an unfavorable impact on the quality of life and the living standards of the whole population.

It should be made clear that the economic blockade is a consequence of the cold war that ended some years ago. Kennedy's pretext for imposing it was based on the developing links between Havana and Moscow, a Cuban alternative to Washington's closed doors and pressure. However, five years ago, those motives ceased to exist and the economic blockade has not only been maintained, but the United States is deliberately and viciously intensifying it, converting it into a war without bombs.

We shall see how this is viewed by two U.S. Congressmen.

George Miller states: "...the embargo is confusing a vendetta with a national interest policy. It's a relic of the cold war...."[61] For his part, Charles Rangel says: "It's time to put an end to the cold war in this hemisphere...."[62]

In a *Washington Post* article published on September 8, 1994, headlined "The Embargo Must End", the presidents of both chambers of the U.S. Congress, Claiborne Pell and Lee Hamilton, comment—in reference to perspectives—that it's time for the U.S. government to begin to think about what the Cuban people really need.[63]

Those who endured World War II or the postwar period will remember the terrible effect of obligatory food rationing, where children and the elderly suffered most. In Cuba, both groups are prioritized but, even so, their quotas of milk and meat have to be reduced to the levels that can be acquired under this unjust measure. People have to go on living pending the arrival

61. ANSA, Washington, March 17, 1994. (Retranslated from Spanish.)
62. Ibid.
63. Claiborne Pell and Lee Hamilton. "The Embargo Must End", in *The Washington Post*, September 8, 1994. (Retranslated from Spanish.)

on time of a freighter carrying cereals that have to be distributed immediately; that is, if the supplies escape U.S. pressures, or if both parties act in secret to avoid the U.S. embassy frustrating the operation. Then there are the long powercuts due to a scarcity of oil, sometimes meaning that cooking has to be done on wood fires for the same reason; seeing children with their toes escaping from worn out shoes without being able to replace them due to an undersupplied national market. While having to suffer these and many other calamities, ranging from a medicine shortage to transportation problems, contemporary Cubans receive the news that the callous U.S. government is tightening the noose even further with what amounts to Spartan stoicism.

The leader of the Cuban Revolution has referred to this issue in these terms: "The economic blockade is much harder, the economic blockade isn't simply the regulations; the economic blockade is the tenacious, unceasing persecution of every commercial operation undertaken by Cuba anywhere."[64]

I

As a general rule, when the United States is planning intervention in another country, it begins by deploying a psychological campaign to convince domestic and international public opinion of the "need" for such an operation. In recent years, it has also been pressuring key countries on the UN Security Council to act according to supposed international interests. The most recent examples of this are the senseless Gulf War, the intervention in Somalia and the occupation of Haiti.

The Voice of America alone comprises 110 transmitters distributed throughout the world, 25 news bureaux for 50 languages, 45 production studios and a modern tel-

64. Fidel Castro Ruz. Speech given at meeting with Pastors for Peace, in *Granma* daily, December 13, 1992, 7.

evision broadcasting and distribution network, in addition to other broadcasts.

Signals from CNN, NBS, CBS, ABC and HBO, wire dispatches from AP and UPI, and U.S. newspapers and magazines have a massive distribution range outside the United States. . . .

U.S. producers control between 60 and 75% of universal television programming, over 50% of cinematic productions and 70% of the global cable flow, thus allowing for that impressive circulation structure to be sustained from within.[65]

It's thus assured that the world will see and hear what the United States wants the world to see and hear. A lie circulated through its media can travel the world as a truth if it's so desired; however, the U.S. population has been prevented from knowing the truth about what is happening in Cuba, in spite of the fact that its presidents have made thousands of speeches on the subject over the last 36 years. No U.S. television networks, magazines or newspapers publish Cuban statements, or if they do, it is only in a fragmented, manipulative context, in order to devaluate them.

This explains why coming into contact with Cuba's realities and discovering that they are the antithesis of what has been absorbed through this propaganda often has a major impact on visitors to the island.

On several occasions, this whole barrage of disinformation or distorted facts has been accompanied by military maneuvers in the periphery of the Cuban archipelago, with the objective of discovering or fabricating a pretext that could facilitate intervention.

65. Leonardo Cano. "Amos de imágenes y palabras" (Masters of Images and Words), in *Granma* daily, August 8, 1994, 7.

Faced with this constant and sustained psychological warfare, the Cuban government has developed an extraordinary dynamism in the diplomatic arena, high-level military preparation for the war of all the people in the case of aggression, and close links with the masses.

II

With the triumph of the Revolution, the popular government set about finding solutions to diverse problems, waging a battle on multiple fronts. The Cuban people immersed themselves in a wide range of tasks, such as eradicating widespread illiteracy and undereducation, in spite of the fact that the United States had carried off the few existing experts and professionals. The country also had to defend itself from daily air aggressions by light aircraft flying out of Miami to raze canefields, bomb economically strategic targets and use indiscriminate strafing attacks on people in the street to sow terror and chaos. In the meantime, agents were also infiltrated to carry out sabotage and attempt to assassinate the head of state.

The people worked to maintain and increase cane production; to diversify agriculture in order to avoid dependency on a single crop; to implement new legislation; to train cadres to provide leadership for the multiple tasks that were required; and to reinforce defense training, given that military aggression appeared imminent. The country didn't sleep; secular backwardness had led to an accumulation of problems that needed immediate confrontation. The time factor was decisive. They were working against the clock.

This incredible panorama was completed by numerous diplomatic, economic and psychological aggressions of every type. Threats, insolence and arrogance were the order of the day.

Enormous efforts in terms of economic and human resources had to be invested to defend the country without abandoning other fronts. Given the situation, it was necessary to simultaneously defend the Revolution and develop the country.

The first ten years saw intensive enemy activity. Cuba lost millions of dollars just in terms of sabotage, defending its borders and repelling U.S. aggressions. Nonetheless, the new Cuban government took on all the tasks needed to improve the life of its people.

The technology employed in Cuba up until 1959—in factories, transportation, agricultural machinery, the sugar industry, etc.—was basically of U.S. origin. Due to the economic blockade, all this equipment was left without spare parts. The country lost further millions of dollars and began to depend on the will and inventiveness of its workers.

The economic link that developed with the Eastern European countries and the Soviet Union in particular was a solution to the problems created in Cuba by the U.S. economic blockade. In this way, considerable momentum could be given to the system's new plans. This obligatory change of market implied a radical technological transformation. Cuba had to start again and change everything, including school books, since even the systems of measure became obsolete. Its commercialization methodology and techniques had to be modified, other languages had to be learned, and new technicians qualified. A tremendous amount of resources were lost in this process.

With the subsequent disappearance of those main suppliers to the Cuban economy for 30 years, not only was the economic blockade intensified but, in a coup de grace, the Torricelli Act was approved. The country remained almost paralyzed while the economy was being reorganized and new markets sought. For five years, with this immoral Act like a noose around its neck and facing relentless and implacable persecution, Cuba, compass in hand, has been attempting to refloat its battered economy in the midst of a hostile sea of unfair prices, difficult payment conditions, no soft credits, markets demanding specific conditions of liquidity, and even higher freight costs—

brought about by greater shipping distances and U.S. sanctions against ships docking in Cuba.

The following data illustrate the financial problems and related economic damage to the Cuban economy brought about by its powerful enemy's hatred. Experts calculate that the 45 billion dollars lost to the island's economy as a consequence of the economic blockade would be sufficient to finance the island's development. This figure is over 20 times Cuba's hard currency income in 1992.

This difficult situation hasn't been reversed, and, as long as the economic blockade remains in force, it will be inevitable.

As Carlos Lage explains:

> Due to price differentials, Cuba paid an excess of up to 41.5 million dollars for grains, chicken and milk in 1992. As for freight costs, it lost more than 85 million dollars; shipping costs for oil were 43% more costly for us and those for other products three times more expensive.

> The illegal freezing of Cuban income from telecommunications stands at over 102 million dollars; in terms of the principal plus the interest due, this figure increases by over seven million dollars per year.

> Cuba received 228,000 U.S. tourists in 1958. At current prices, this tourist presence would represent an income of approximately 200 million dollars to the country.

> If Cuba maintained just one third of its former sugar exports to the U.S. market, which paid 21.30 cents a pound for sugar in 1992, the income from this sector would have been 205 million dollars higher.

> By having to sell its sugar on the residual market because of the economic blockade, Cuba is losing a potential income of 39 million dollars.

By being forced to use currency other than the U.S. dollar in international financial operations as a consequence of the economic blockade, Cuba is losing millions of dollars.

Lacking soft credits, the country is forced into accepting much more costly and shorter-term trade credits.

U.S. pressures on foreign investors wishing to do business with Cuba, is stemming a potentially considerable flow of investment. Nine out of every ten business attempts are foiled by U.S. pressure.[66]

In 1993, every ton of milk imported from Europe cost 80 dollars; with this amount of money, we could have acquired 2-2.3 tons through access to the subsidized U.S. market. . . .

That is to say, the Cuban people [for whom this vital product is rationed] failed to drink 55 million glasses of milk (in 1993 alone).[67]

The ban on sales of medical products to the island is yet another of the economic blockade's negative consequences. For example, in Cuba, 16.5 per 1,000 inhabitants (some 200, 000 people) are dependent on insulin. Ely Lilly Canada Inc., which manufactures this drug, is a subsidiary of the world's main insulin producer, a U.S. company. Under the Torricelli Act, the Canadian company has been forced to suspend sales to the island.

66. Mario Vázquez Raña. Interview granted by Carlos Lage, secretary of the Executive Committee of the Council of Ministers, to *El Sol de México*, in *Granma* daily, May 29, 1993, 6.
67. "La lista negra de Washington" (Washington's Blacklist), in *Bohemia* magazine, August 19, 1994, 37.

Adults and children with heart complaints are often dependent on pacemakers to relieve suffering or even to save their lives. Cuba's traditional suppliers—from whom Cuba purchased some 600 of these devices per year at approximately 1,000 dollars per unit—were the Siemens company of Sweden and Teratronics of Australia. The Australian pacemakers, although containing U.S. components, were sold to Cuba through third countries to avoid Washington's displeasure; but when the parent company opened offices in the United States, it was told to stop supplying the vital devices to Cuba. The company couldn't withstand the pressure.

In July 1994, Siemens informed Cuba in an official letter, signed in the Swedish capital by Maria Cristina Rosell, that its pacemaker division had been sold to the U.S. St. Jude Medical Inc. St. Paul, a company deferring to the immoral measures—or so-called embargo—that the United States has maintained against Cuba for over 30 years.[68]

Other sectors of the economy are experiencing similar problems:

> The Swiss Fulka Chemical Company Ltd., which produces chemical reagents and other agents for radiology laboratories; British Railpower Ltd., which builds locomotive diesel engines for the sugar cane industry; and the H.J. Heinz Company of Canada Ltd., have informed their Cuban buyers that they are unable to fulfill their commitments, having been refused permission to do so by the U.S. Treasury Department.[69]

> Alimport [the cuban food import enterprise] is carrying losses of 70 million dollars per year as a result of the official U.S. persecution in Venezuela . . . of companies sell-

68. Pedro Prada. "El laberinto del minotauro" (The Labyrinth of the Minotaur), in *Bohemia* magazine, August 19, 1994, 34.
69. Nidia Díaz. Op. cit.

ing frozen chicken to Cuba and similar activity against powdered milk suppliers in Spain.[70]

In 1993, Cuba's foreign trade losses alone approached one billion dollars.

Sufficient material exists to compile a book of all these massive violations of the human rights of 11 million Cuban inhabitants.

In numerous cases the United States has threatened other countries with refusing to buy particular machinery, equipment or parts that contains Cuban nickel. Exactly the same thing happens if a product contains Cuban sugar.

It has been explicitly stated in the U.S. Congress that the object of these measures is to facilitate a corrosive process from below, using food shortages and the deterioration of the Cuban health system to make the country ungovernable.

Any sensible person can see that such behavior is clearly misanthropic or psychopathic. The U.S. government cannot accept that a people can attain social gains without resorting to violent public demonstrations to defend its most elemental rights, or that the Cuban government has never used tear gas or curfews to repress its people for demanding jobs, health care, education, social security or other basic rights. Only psychopaths could be annoyed by the fact that there is one Third World country that doesn't have the dismal panorama presented by the Organization of American States (OAS) in the following study:

> At least 115 million children in the Americas live in conditions of extreme poverty and in situations of acute exploitation, with frequent cases of murder, torture and sexual abuse. This heartrending report was presented by the Inter-American Human Rights Commission to the 23rd session of the OAS General Assembly, held in Managua, Nicaragua, in June 1993.

70. Pedro Prada. Op. cit., 35.

The text explains that 45% of the region's 440 million inhabitants are children, the majority of whom live in "conditions of extreme poverty." "It is estimated that approximately 115 million minors are affected by multiple shortages resulting from poverty," the report notes. "There are frequent cases of murder, torture and exploitation of every kind, sexual abuse, abandonment, and the use of children as involuntary organ donors, in sales and in prostitution." At the same time, it warns of increasing numbers of children caught up in drug addiction and substance abuse, "an affront to the dignity and integrity of minors in the hemisphere."

According to the Inter-American Human Rights Commission, streetchildren . . . comprise a large army of victims of exploitation by those who take advantage of their homeless situation. The Commission warned of the grave phenomenon of the so-called Brazilian "death squads" that are murdering streetchildren in mass "social cleansing" operations.

The report noted that these death squads are paid by merchants or business associations to get rid of these streetchildren by shooting them in the head in cold blood.

According to UN figures, Brazil has some 12 million streetchildren, the majority in Rio de Janeiro, São Paulo and Recife, cities where dozens of bodies of murdered children have been found in garbage dumps.

There are some 50,000 street urchins in Colombia, organized in street communes and surviving by pillaging. In other countries of the continent, such as Guatemala, Peru, Nicaragua and El Salvador, the violence and murder meted out to streetchildren is equally shameful, the report adds. The Commission confirmed the existence of "a cruel reality," fomented by factors of extreme poverty, marginality, abandonment and lack of resources, making it impossible "to assure citizens in the hemisphere, from an early age, of the enjoyment of their most elemental right to life and physical integrity."[71]

This leads one to doubt Mr. Gore's sincerity in saying that Cuban literacy successes are a cause for shame. At the same time, one has to doubt Hillary Clinton's complaints when she laments the deterioration of a health care system that condemns U.S. citizens to severe suffering, and one would also have to doubt President Clinton's criticisms of the forces that frustrated his health care program in Congress.

III

Cuban agriculture was dependent on 1.3 billion tons of fertilizer per year and suddenly found itself without any; the 13 million tons of petroleum that fuelled the country were abruptly reduced to less than half that figure; the eight billion dollars in annual imports fell to less than two billion in one year; the domestic market was emptied of supplies and the country's purchasing power was reduced by approximately 70%.[72]

The lack of oil—formerly purchased at the rate of one ton of sugar for eight tons of oil, current prices standing at one ton of sugar for 1.4 tons of oil—has affected innumerable plans for the construction of housing, schools, day-care centers, dairy plants, irrigation channels, dams, and agricultural projects, among others.

It was a rude shock for the country, immersed at the time in a feverish rhythm of work, to have to suspend or postpone,

71. *World Almanac 1994*, 187.
72. Mario Vázquez Raña. Op.cit. and Carlos Lage during his television appearance on the program "Hoy Mismo", in *Granma* daily, November 10, 1992, 3.

modify or limit many of those projects, to make vital priority adjustments and to renounce accelerated development. The debacle in Eastern Europe, combined with the U.S. economic blockade and its complement, the Torricelli Act, forced Cuba into adopting more modest goals. Oxen were substituted for tractors, with a resultant drop in agricultural production; many people had to be encouraged to work in the country's rural areas, because advanced technology and mechanization combined with ample open-access educational opportunities had stimulated an exodus of young campesinos in the direction of other areas and professions. This has led to a contemporary rural population of only 20%. Mechanization is on hold for better times, or until the fuel and spare parts become available.

The country has the capacity to store over 10 billion cubic meters of water in large and small reservoirs. These are stocked with fry and currently produce some 25,000 tons of fish per year, with prospects of reaching 100,000 tons.

The country continues to produce—on a lesser scale due to the lack of raw materials—some agricultural machinery and transportation and medical equipment. Also significant is the industrial production of new medicines obtained from biotechnological and genetic engineering methods, a sector that has attained significant development in Cuba.

The huge areas planted with citrus fruits, among the most important in the world, also depended heavily on imported supplies. With supreme efforts, creativity and labor, Cuba is fighting to maintain them.

The Cuban regime had planned to provide a staggered solution to the real problem of housing. To this end, a plan had been drawn up for the construction of approximately 100,000 housing units per year. This objective was close to target when the socialist bloc collapsed, to be followed by the tightening of the U.S. economic blockade. No other government in the world had ever come close to taking on such a challenge.

This aspiration was not utopian; to achieve this goal, Cuba embarked on the difficult task of creating part of the infrastructure that was needed, fundamentally the construction materials factories. The country was very close to achieving its aims when the unexpected happened. In spite of these difficult times, new low-cost housing technology has been created, using new materials such as Roman cement. Although the country had developed a cement industry capable of producing six million tons, fuel shortages meant that factories were unable to function.

Work on the Juraguá nuclear plant, Cuba's hoped-for solution to most of its energy needs, had to be stopped when it was 85% completed.

IV

This is the second time in 35 years that Cuba has had to change its entire technology, markets and commercial structure. A Third World country, underdeveloped, lacking credits and international funding of any kind and economically blockaded on top of all that, Cuba is losing billions of dollars urgently needed for its development, the consequence of undemocratic measures imposed by the country that regards itself as the champion of democracy.

The Eastern European debacle resulted in the loss of a genuinely equitable trade pricing system, labelled as "Russian subsidies" by Cuba's enemies and Washington propaganda. These prices made it possible to invest an annual 30% of the gross domestic product (GDP) in the country's development, over the course of 25 years. In order to fully grasp the magnitude of this development, it should be recalled that developed countries such as Great Britain, Germany, France and the United States were investing only 1% of their GDP in development. At that time, manufactured goods, agricultural equipment, transportation and industry cost 30, 40 or 50 times less than their current prices. The whole Cuban strategy employed to achieve the accelerated development that was successfully being reached had to be modified. However, enemy expectations of the country's collapse were not fulfilled.

That deliberate U.S. interference designed to frustrate the development plans of a country whose only sin consisted in fighting to pull its people out of secular backwardness and offer them a better and more humane world, can only be described as a crime against humanity. The international community has a responsibility not just to support petitions for the lifting of the economic blockade, but to take those responsible to the International Court of Justice to secure the minimal demand of compensation for all the material damage that this measure—condemned on three occasions in the UN General Assembly—has wreaked on Cuba's development. This kind of crime could be committed against any Latin American country deciding to adopt democratic measures more aligned to the needs of our peoples.

The responsible investment of significant resources to aid the country's development made it possible for Cuba to improve living standards and to create the necessary infrastructure for the country's opening to foreign capital, while maintaining a nationalist path. Foreign investors recognize that Cuban industry has the necessary requirements for its competitive insertion into the global market, on account of its modernity, the professional and educational levels of its personnel and the security offered by a drug-free and non-violent society. Even the U.S. business community can point to Cuba as one of the safest countries in terms of foreign investment. The U.S. magazine *Political Risk Services* gives it 29th place.

Cuba's high standard of living has declined in the last five years as a consequence of what Cubans call the "double blockade", that is, the loss of the beneficial trade and financial agreements with Eastern Europe and the effects of the United States' Cuba policy.

It's no secret that, in the period 1990-1993, 11 of Cuba's principal agricultural sectors nose-dived, as in the case of livestock, which declined by 70%, while industrial food production (sugar, dairy products and canned goods) experienced a similar decline.

Those losses gave rise to a perceptible reduction in per capita calorie intake and dietary variation, together with a 50% affectation in terms of nutritional intake.

Notwithstanding, those levels are not inferior to those recorded in the country prior to 1959, when over half the population lacked an income source and thus was unable to acquire the most basic foods. . . .

The FAO has noted that the country's food supply situation, although serious, is of a temporary nature and is being dealt with through equitable distribution and the authorities' efforts to overcome the economic crisis.[73]

UNESCO likewise "recently confirmed that the economic blockade of Cuba decreed by the United States is seriously affecting education, science, culture and communications and thus causing severe damage to Cubans' spirituality."[74]

The economic blockade hinders the acquisition of resources needed to maintain Cuba's educational and professional training systems, crucial for such "spiritual" satisfaction.

Shortages of reagents, equipment and other resources have reduced laboratory tests to zero and damaged the quality of studies in chemistry, physics, biology and mathematics, in addition to other specialized subjects such as

73. "Cuba hoy" (Cuba Today), in *Bohemia* magazine, September 30, 1994, 4.
74. Pedro Prada. "Bloqueo, almas en cerco" (The Blockade, Souls Under Siege), in *Bohemia* magazine, September 30, 1994, 4.

microbiology, pharmaceuticals, nutrition, soil, computer science, informatics and automation.[75]

The print run of book publications dropped from approximately 20,000 to 2,000 or 3,000 per title. One significant piece of information is that prior to the collapse of the socialist bloc, Cuba published as many books per 100,000 inhabitants as the United States, according to the *World Almanac 1994*, without counting the hundreds that were acquired already printed. (See Table 5.)

Cuban literature is banned in the United States, and published material from the United States cannot be sent to Cuba, except for political tracts glorifying U.S. society and demonizing the Cuban system.

The United States also denies visas to Cubans needing to travel to that country, even in the case of work reasons. Scientists invited to offer papers at the 1993 meeting of the American Nuclear Society found themselves in that category, as did the inventors of the Cuban meningitis vaccine, and the Cuban ballet dancers invited to perform at the Oscar awards ceremony. Cuban folklore singer Merceditas Valdés was denied entry into the United States in 1994, and the musical group Mezcla filed a suit against the U.S authorities for the same reason. A number of prestigious Cuban artists have also been unable to charge for performances or receive prizes because of this ban.[76]

Numerous U.S. celebrities have risked disobeying their government's restrictions to visit Cuba. These include actor and songwriter Harry Belafonte, Jane Fonda, Arnold Schwarzeneger, Oliver Stone, Dizzy Gillespie, Carmine Coppola, Francis Ford Coppola, Graham Greene, Robert Redford, Sidney Pollack, Robert de Niro, Holly Near, and Igor Yuzkevitch, as well as many other artists, scientists, workers and professionals.

75. Ibid, 5-6.
76. "Departamento de Estado a tribunales por negar visa a músicos cubanos" (Lawsuit Against State Department for Denying Visas to Cuban Musicians), in *Granma* daily, May 25, 1994, 4.

The economic blockade has caused millions of dollars' worth of damage in the cultural field. Sabotage and pressures on third countries are widespread. Although it seems ridiculous, Cubans are also officially banned from viewing U.S. movies.

To an extent, the measures applied against Cuba have been exposed to the world and the truth has gained ground, initially among the most aware and then gradually among others. This has resulted in the beginnings of a more widespread condemnation of those immoral measures.

Members of the upper class or bourgeois sectors—apart from a few exceptions—will not make public criticism of U.S. policies towards Cuba for fear of damaging their interests. However, many people throughout the world are rejecting the methods applied by the United States against Cuba and, even though they might disagree with the model chosen by the Cubans because it conflicts with their class interests, they sympathize with the country's plight, perceiving the economic blockade as a genocidal, immoral and illegal act.

Although the military balance between the "two worlds" disappeared with the extinction of the socialist bloc, a new correlation, derived from the unjust restrictions imposed on the Cuban people, has made an appearance: a correlation of sympathy in favor of the indomitable island and increased antipathy to Washington's anti-Cuba and genocidal policies, leaving the United States in true moral isolation.

All over the world—and particularly among U.S. citizens—numerous groups have sprung up, merging together in a militant manner to constitute genuine fighting movements condemning the illegal economic blockade, and demanding respect for Cuba's sovereign right as an independent nation to choose the socioeconomic system that its people consider most appropriate for the country's development.

This defense of Cuba's self-determination is based on irrefutable arguments.

Article 3, clause b) of the OAS Charter states: "International order is essentially constituted by a respect for the character, sovereignty and independence of states."[77] Clause c) affirms that "Every state has the right to choose its own political, economic and social system and to organize itself in the way it considers most appropriate, without external interference, and has a duty not to interfere in the affairs of another state."[78]

Page 29 of *¿Qué es la democracia?* asserts the official U.S. stance that democratic governments have come to equally accept both the most dedicated socialists and partisans of the free market.[79] For President Clinton, this policy has been respected in the cases of China, North Korea and Viet Nam, but in the case of Cuba, "the circumstances are different,"[80] Yet not one member of the cabinet, nor the president himself, has clarified where the difference lies.

Article 12 of the same regional charter reads: "States have the right . . . to organize themselves as they see fit."[81]

And in article 18:

> No state or group of states has the right to directly or indirectly intervene, for any reason, in the internal or external affairs of any other . . . or employ any form of interference or aggressive tendency that poses a threat to the nature of a state, or against the political, economic and cultural elements that constitute it."[82]

77. Ángel Fernández-Rubio. "Carta de la Organización de Estados Americanos" (Charter of the Organization of American States), in *Instrumentos jurídicos internacionales* (International Legal Instruments), Chap. 2, p. 828. (Retranslated from Spanish.)
78. Ibid.
79. Howard Cincotta. Op. cit., 29.
80. AP. Washington, August 19, 1994. (Retranslated from Spanish.)
81. Ángel Fernández-Rubio. Op. cit., 830. (Retranslated from Spanish.)
82. Ibid, 831.

In addition, Article 2 of the UN Charter makes it clear that "All members shall refrain in their international relations from the threat or use of force against the territorial integrity or political independence of any state."[83]

Armed with this legal basis and Cuba's social achievements —in spite of all the outside obstacles—solidarity organizations are taking the floor to defend a system in which they can perceive a solution to their own problems, daily aggravated by the incompetency of neoliberal models imposed on them by a decadent capitalism.

This defense is not just a theoretical one: with untiring and growing activity, those groups working in solidarity with Cuba have collected—and continue to collect—a huge quantity of material resources, medicines, pencils, notebooks, wheelchairs, computers and many other items, to help alleviate to a small extent the terrible shortages provoked by the restrictions. Without a doubt, U.S. aggression towards Cuba has been precisely the best generator of solidarity and the formation of such organizations.

The millions of men and women who hold this altruistic attitude towards Cuba evaluate the problem as a moral, ethical and humane issue that goes beyond narrow political criteria; after all, the economic blockade equally affects religious believers, atheists, black, white and mixed race Cubans, women, men, children, senior citizens, all members of society. For this reason, the solidarity movements have two fundamental demands:

- That the UN General Assembly resolutions on the lifting of the economic blockade imposed on Cuba by the United States be unconditionally respected.

83. Charter of the United Nations. *The Europa Year Book.*

- That all the agreements, charters, treaties and the regulations governing international law in relation to the principles of self-determination and non-interference in the internal affairs of other states be respected.

As part of the vital restructuring of its economy as a consequence of the double blockade, Cuba has been forced to find urgent alternatives. Solidly rejecting any return to a market economy—with its shock policies that leave millions of workers without employment or protection—it is putting into practice new options that permit the country's continued development and the preservation of its social conquests. These decisions—supported by the people, while defending a principled position—also take into account that the powerful enemy to the north has not given up its objective of crushing the Cuban Revolution. Of course, given Washington's implacable antipathy and enmity, Cuba's way is not an easy one.

The backbone of the new Cuban economic focus is based on the formation of joint ventures with foreign investors able to contribute what the country lacks (or the economic blockade prevents it from obtaining), such as markets, raw materials, supplies, financing or a marketing structure for the sale of Cuban products overseas. This variant is radically different from those neoliberal policies where a country's heritage is sold through ill-fated privatizations, with disastrous effects on its workers and on the already impoverished domestic economies of the underdeveloped countries.

In order to guarantee a rapid investment recovery, quick dividends and wide contact with the outside world, an equivalent to breaking the information blockade, the Cuban leadership decided to prioritize developing its tourist industry. On the one hand, Cuba has optimum natural conditions, a well-developed construction infrastructure, and a highly qualified work force with impressive cultural and academic standards; on the other hand, it offers security, public order and social and political stability. These conditions make the country a very attractive location for investment in this sector.

Encouraging results have been obtained within a few years and the country already receives up to 800,000 tourists per year, to whom it can offer a wide range of options, including the innovation of health tourism.

Table 11

UN General Assembly Voting in Favor of Lifting the U.S. Economic Blockade of Cuba

Date	Resolution	Total of countries	In favor	Abstained	Against
November 24, 1992	47/19	133	59	71	U.S. Israel Romania
October 3, 1993	48/16	149	88	57	U.S. Israel Albania Paraguay
October 26, 1994	-	151	101	48	U.S. Israel

SOURCE: Compiled by the author from data taken from: "Abrumadora mayoría aprueba Resolución contra el bloqueo" ("Overwhelming Majority Approves Resolution Against Blockade), by Roberto Molina, *Granma* daily, Havana, October 27, 1994.

SINGLE PARTY SYSTEM VS SINGLE PARTY SYSTEM

The Cuban Revolutionary Party embodies the Cuban people.
—José Martí

The genesis of the Cuban Party is the result of the union of all the forces that took part in the overthrow of the Batista tyranny: the July 26 Movement, the March 13 Revolutionary Directorate and the Popular Socialist Party, all of which subsequently made up the Integrated Revolutionary Organizations (ORI). The imminent threat of an aggression from abroad accelerated the integration of these forces, given the urgent need for unity. The ORI became the United Party of the Socialist Revolution: a single party to confront the aggression of an also single and very powerful enemy. Martí, through his Cuban Revolutionary Party, confronted Spanish colonialism, a formidable power a that time, and Bolívar, Juárez and San Martín would have done the same, just as any contemporary strategist would do, this being elementary common sense.

As a result of an increase in foreign aggression and the virtual state of siege imposed on the country, the Cuban system rapidly became radical and the democratic-bourgeois revolution was transformed into a socialist revolution and the standard-bearer of the Communist Party of Cuba (PCC).

An interesting aspect is that this decision was not made by a small group of individuals, but by the determination of all the people who, no longer afraid of words and epithets, embraced the essence of the epoch's most advanced ideas.

The statutes of this new party were drawn up after a broad discussion by all its members, making it a very selective but not sectarian vanguard organization. Membership requirements—human, moral and ethical quality, loyalty and fidelity to the homeland, solidarity, a spirit of sacrifice, integrity and honesty—make it possible to guarantee a clear path for the struggle to reach its noble objectives. The Communist Party of Cuba's acceptance of believers and religious people is an important distinguishing trait with respect to other similar parties.

The Cuban people know that unity in battle is a sure sign of success. This is why they do not deny, but honestly and courageously proclaim, assume and establish the need for a single party.

A brief analysis of the two parties which take turns at power in the United States is sufficient to understand the Cubans' position.

The Republican and Democratic Parties in the United States were born as twins, from the same egg. Perhaps as a result of the ideas of Plato—who attributed them to Socrates and stated that democracy and republic had the same identity— they started to appear as a single party. In the *World Almanac 1968* it is said: "Jefferson was an agrarian, an expansionist, because he opposed the federalists and centralization. He was called a Republican, now synonymous with Democrat."[84]

Eisenhower, a Republican, was behind the idea of and directed the mercenary invasion of Cuba. That same head of government overthrew Guatemalan President Jacobo Arbenz when he was carrying out changes which benefitted his people.

The Democrat Kennedy did not modify his Republican predecessor's plan; on the contrary, he assumed and perfected it to launch the invasion against the young Cuban Revolution. He also supported the Saigon puppet regime, an interference which a year later would propitiate the cruel war against the Vietnamese people.

The Democrat Johnson—who succeeded Kennedy—escalated hostility against Cuba. He invaded the Dominican Republic, supported Israel's pirate actions against the Arab countries and its occupation of the east bank of the Sinai, the Golan Heights, the West Bank and the Gaza Strip. Just as his pre-

84. *World Almanac 1968*, 196.

decessors, he maintained, abetted and supported all existing military tyrannies, and using as a pretext the self-aggression in the Gulf of Tonkin he unleashed the Viet Nam war.

Nixon, a Republican, was no different from former presidents. He tightened the economic blockade against Cuba, strengthened his support for Israel and escalated the war in Southeast Asia. Later on he was forced to resign because of the Watergate scandal.

The Republican Reagan maintained a harmonious coherence in the aggressive policy inaugurated by his coreligionist Eisenhower and continued by Democrats and Republicans. He was responsible for the chronic virulence against Cuba. To demonstrate to the powerful economic groups making up his country's real power that they could confide in him, he invaded Grenada and betrayed Latin America when he took sides with Great Britain in the Malvinas war, despite the Treaty for Reciprocal Assistance, by virtue of which Washington committed itself to defend any of our hemisphere's countries if they were attacked by an extracontinental power.

Another Republican, Bush, maintained the policy of hostilities against Cuba and increased it to unprecedented heights by taking advantage of the circumstances that placed Cuba in a critical position, when as a consequence of the disappearance of the socialist bloc and the collapse of the Soviet Union it was left without suppliers and without a market for its products. So as not to be left behind in his antidemocratic emulation of his predecessors, he invaded Panama and committed there all types of misdeeds that went against international law, bilateral treaties, the Charter of the Organization of American States (OAS) and the Charter of the United Nations (UN). Some of these misdeeds are known and others are not, since the U.S. media established a blockade on all other information media. For example, common graves are still being discovered that perhaps contain ten times as many victims as those declared at the time by the White House. This president also committed the inhuman attack on Iraq—where they practiced the same method of disinformation—when that country did to Kuwait the same as the United States did to Grenada, Panama, Haiti, Puerto Rico, Nicaragua and the Philippines, and what Israel, its partner in crime in the Middle East, has done on numerous occasions: invading a neighboring territory.

Is it necessary to recall that it was a Democrat, Mr. Truman, who—almost at the end of World War II—dropped the two unnecessary atomic bombs on Japan? It was that same Democrat who created the North Atlantic Treaty Organization (NATO), attacked Korea and, not by chance—perhaps to solidify his country's hegemonic spirit, as reflected in the slogan "America for the Americans"—founded in our continent the OAS.

Can it be assured that the U.S. Republican Party is innocent with relation to this policy and the 200,000 dead left in the wake of the atomic bombing of Hiroshima and Nagasaki?

The current Democratic president, Bill Clinton, invaded Haiti—this was the second time in this century that the U.S. government invaded this country—on the threshold of the 21st century, counter to the majority of world public opinion and that of his own people. And so that there be no doubt as to his hegemonic positions, Clinton threatened the world with the use of force whenever the United States feels compelled to do so.[85]

It is not necessary to lay bare the antidemocratic and totalitarian nature of these two parties. Their own actions contradict the purported existence of a democratic, multi-party system.

All this demonstrates that, in reality, there is only one party in the United States: the *demorepublican* party, which at the moment is wearing the right wing Democrat's hat and tomorrow may switch to the ultra-right wing Republican's. The use of different names only serves to confuse the public and con-

85. PL, Havana, September 26, 1994.

ceal the fact that the only party that really exists is called economic power and has its headquarters in Wall Street.

A two-party system which in practice has an absolute affinity with aggressive, interventionist, arrogant, hegemonic, irresponsible and brazen policies is equivalent to an unmistakable one-party system whose actions are more identified with international gangsterism and crime than with a model of democracy. It is impossible to identify democracy with interventions, plunder, threats, blackmail, injustice, crime, lies, betrayal and exploitation. Senator Sanders himself calls it an oligarchy. This is the utterly undemocratic history of a nation whose House of Representatives has had a Democratic majority for the past 40 years.

Faced with these facts, there is no doubt that there is no country or continent that when divided can confront a power with such an hegemonic philosophy. Despite Latin America's ideological diversity and pluralistic character, it has an infinite number of common interests around which it is necessary to unite to be able to dream of a better future. This genuine potential for integration, demonstrated at the four Ibero-American Summits, are a real headache for U.S. plutocrats. They are convinced that Latin American unity is a grave threat to their hegemonic control. Thus the fierce questioning of the existence of a single party in Cuba, as if only one approach were possible in Latin America.

The holding of a summit in Miami without Cuba's participation was clear proof of the United States' intentions to keep the continent divided. In this way Wall Street can be united against a weak Latin America. This demonstrates that they recognize Cuba as being a unifying element.

They attempt to alienate us by not acknowledging our cultural and historical identity, bombarding us with foreign and superficial models, inoculating us with a canned Coca-Cola "culture" to impose false aesthetic, ethical and historical values. The reason behind this is to distance us from our rich heritage, history and culture, where we can find the tactics and strategy we must use to emerge victorious in this unequal battle.

Simón Bolívar once stated: "If my death contributes to the end of parties and the consolidation of the Union, I will peacefully go to my grave."[86]

José Martí understood this very well. For him, unity around a single party was the key to success and he wasn't wrong: he founded the Cuban Revolutionary Party and achieved the defeat of the Spaniards, although later on victory was snatched away by U.S. intervention.

History has taught us other lessons: the Vietnamese people first defeated the French and then the U.S. armed forces, the North Koreans defeated Truman's forces and the Soviet people defeated the terrible Nazi army; all of them did this with a single party. The Cuban model of democracy, also having a single party, has won for itself a place in the world which is bigger than the one it had before 1959 as a U.S. neocolony, when it had several parties.

In Latin America the panorama has changed: the governments which obey Washington's orders no longer hold a majority. Many of them have inevitably started to compare Cuba's successes with the failure of the neoliberal formula in their countries. Some of them are already showing interest in Cuban methods and alternatives. Our continent's leaders are worried about the destiny of our peoples. That is, we have advanced a little and this is confirmed by the Ibero-American Summits.

It is true that there is not an absolute unity of opinion on core problems, because there still isn't a full awareness of the strength provided by unity. It is also true that there is a lack of strong language and a resistance to calling things by their real name. Neither is it fully clear what tactic and strategy to fol-

86. Felipe Larrazábal. *La vida y correspondencia general del Libertador Simón Bolívar* (The Life and Correspondence of the Liberator Simón Bolívar), 2: 567.

low. But it is also true that many Latin American patriots have some knowledge of the continent's history and know about Bolívar's objectives on convening the Panama Congress without the presence of the United States. Anyone can see in the Ibero-American Summits the essence of the Liberator's dreams when he launched the idea of the Amphictyonic Congress.

Our solidarity with Cuba movements have been created with the purpose of demanding from our governments that they adopt a position towards the United States corresponding with the UN General Assembly decision on the economic blockade. It has also been demanded that they be more consistent at the Ibero-American Summits to accelerate the integration process. We could also demand that the first point on the agenda of the next U.S.-organized summit should be that our governments pressure this nation to practice what it mistakenly (with good or dubious intentions) has been demanding from Cuba: a democratic opening. Or to practice what its own democratic postulates proclaim: that it respect plurality, that it comply with the principle of noninterference established by international law, that in accordance with the UN Charter and the OAS Charter it respect the Cuban people's right to choose the sociopolitical system that best suits its interests without any interference, that it not lose sight of Juárez' principle of respect for the rights of others so that there can be peace.

As we can see, these demands are based on the most elemental internationally established norms of coexistence; they are petitions that humiliate no one. It is hypocritical to strangle a socioeconomic system without giving it a chance to develop and then declare that it didn't work.

Our struggle's immediate goal should be to oppose Wall Street's single party system with a single Latin American party system. We must combat Washington's "divide and conquer" tactics with the Latin American philosophy that "unity is strength". In this way we can demand an end to the economic blockade and ask that Cuba be materially indemnified for all damages suffered, calculated at approximately 45 billion dollars.

As a result of the absence of that unity, so necessary and urgent, our continent is threatened by a political, social and economic cost with even graver consequences. Let no one doubt that faced with the irrefutable failure of neoliberalism, our common enemy will resort again to the alternative of military tyrannies. This option is based on the need to maintain the U.S. military-industrial complex—which guarantees jobs for 170,000 workers and revenues of 23 billion dollars. It is also based on Bill Clinton's recent speech at the last session of the UN General Assembly, where he corroborated his government's role as world police force.

To be able to evaluate the significance and importance of unity, just imagine the U.S. leaders' reaction if at a negotiating table or at a Miami Summit they were to face a united Latin America demanding that the foreign debt be forgiven. Can anyone imagine what would happen if all of a sudden a united Latin America, acting like one single nation, were to refuse to export its products to the United States?

NAPOLEONIC ARROGANCE

We love Lincoln's homeland as much as we fear Cutting's homeland.

—José Martí

It is worthwhile setting aside a chapter to talk about the United States' position and attitude and the language used by its leaders when referring to our peoples and specifically to Cuba and its president. For them it is normal practice to adopt a vulgar, arrogant and insolent stance in relations with nations whose citizens they consider to be inferior beings coming from inferior countries. Unfortunately, this dishonorable stance is marring the noble task of that country's founding fathers. The United States' conduct in no way resembles traditional British respect, the proverbial consideration of French diplomacy, the Europeans' high concept of relations between countries, or Asian honorability. Italy, Germany, the Netherlands, Austria, Australia, Canada, and Third World countries show respect for the Caribbean island, as its people deserve, and Cuba reciprocates this respect. The only government which wants to bring Martí's homeland down on its knees uses an irreverent and vulgar language unworthy of the history of a nation which fought for its independence and sovereignty basing itself on truly democratic postulates. Far from exalting, ill treatment belittles those who practice it, just as hate damages those who engender it.

As I read the rosary of foolish imperial remarks appearing in a speech given by the U.S. under-secretary of state for Inter-American affairs, Alexander Watson, on October 26, 1993, two possibilities came to mind: either this gentleman is a relative of the families who benefitted from the billion dollars that the United States stole from Cuba between 1950-1960, or he fell asleep in his fiefdom in the Middle Ages and woke up in 1993 after dreaming that one of his serfs had stolen his property, consisting in an island in the Caribbean.

Even though it is a waste of time trying to list all the foolish things the secretary said, it is worthwhile, however, to stop at a part of his speech where he refers to what President Clinton said:

> I don't think the United States can maintain normal relations with any country that has strayed from democracy, Cuba being one of them. With respect to Cuba, our objective is to promote a peaceful transition to democracy. We believe the Cuban people deserve to be free so they can decide their own future, expressed through their will in free elections.[87]

If Napoleon had given this speech it would have been more coherent. Spoken by a Democrat, the president of a country which shares the postulates of the UN Charter, the Charter of the Organization of American States and international law, by virtue of which it is obliged to respect the self-determination of nations, it is absolutely incomprehensible.

It is an interesting fact that the United States maintains relations with the People's Republic of China—a country which does not meet Washington's parameters for a democratic nation—and to top it off gives it most favored nation treatment.

The same goes for Viet Nam, where the United States lost tens of thousands of its soldiers in an unjust war which it unleashed. It maintained relations with the USSR for many years, as well as with all the socialist bloc countries, and neither did they fall under Washington's category of democratic countries. If Cuba is following the same development model as that chosen by the peoples of Viet Nam and China, why is the United States set on giving it different treatment?

---

87. Alexander Watson. Speech given before the Cuban American National Foundation, October 26, 1993. (Retranslated from Spanish.)

It is disconcerting that the reasoning of the head of the biggest world power is so base, arrogant and unprofessional. According to him, the circumstances are not the same. However, not even the president or any of his cabinet's officials has been able to explain what the difference is in these circumstances. Neither have they been able to provide the name of the international organization which has given them the authority to assume that their objective in Cuba is to promote a peaceful transition to democracy. What is clear is that the UN General Assembly has called on the United States to lift its unilateral economic blockade on the island. Moreover, the U.S. president himself confesses to at times being alone in his endeavor to overthrow Castro.

Furthermore, what right does President Clinton have to consider what the Cuban people—or any other, for that matter—are worthy of? What right does the president of the United States have to judge whether a political model is democratic or not? In a civilized country governed by international law and the agreements that regulate relations among states, this conduct represents not only a lack of respect but also interference in the internal affairs of other countries. A country that deliberately and systematically violates another country's radiophonic space to insult, slander and try to destabilize a government elected by popular consensus cannot speak of democracy.

On the other hand, did the United States recognize as democratic the governments of Pinochet, Stroessner, Somoza, Batista, Duvalier, Trujillo, Ríos Mont, or those imposed by military coups in Argentina, Brazil, Guatemala or El Salvador? It isn't necessary to convince anyone of the antidemocratic character of those bloodthirsty military regimes. However, not only did Washington not break relations with those tyrants, but it gave them protection, and their most infamous torturers were trained in U.S. academies. Do there exist more normal relations than those of the United States with all those tyrannies that had openly abandoned the democratic model?

It's a shame that because of his age, President Clinton cannot remember the military coups and bloody totalitarian tyrannies that proliferated in Latin America between 1950 and 1982. For example, in Argentina there was General Eduardo Leonardi, who overthrew Perón, a president elected by universal suffrage. Tyrannies such as those of Onganía, Levinton, and Lanusse made their appearance between 1966 and 1973. In 1976, General Videla also overthrew a democratically elected government, that of Mrs. Perón. Another general, Roberto Viola, came to power and was replaced by Horacio Liendo, and then it was General Galtieri's turn. As tyrannies became outmoded, in 1983 General Bignone called for elections. That is why it doesn't surprise us when we read a Prensa Latina news dispatch datelined Buenos Aires reporting on President Carlos Menem's expulsion from the Human Rights Permanent Assembly, of which he was the honorary president. It was precisely this Argentine president who pardoned and vindicated the main military leaders who had been condemned by courts of justice on five occasions for their actions between 1976 and 1983 when they did away with the Constitution and all the country's laws, leaving in their wake 30, 000 disappeared—apart from the tortured and murdered.

Was it any different in Bolivia? The list of generals is also long: Barrientos overthrew a government elected by the people, and it was during his reign that Che Guevara was murdered—with the complicity of U.S. agents. The Bolivian people angrily remember those who were murdered or disappeared during the autocratic governments of Generals Ovando, Hugo Banzer, García Meza and Torrelio Villa and the military junta.

Honduras, Guatemala, El Salvador, Paraguay and so many others have such similar histories that it would seem as if they had occurred in one country. This is not a coincidence, for they bear the same stamp: that of Washington.

Just as Menem tries to protect the henchmen of former tyrannies; just as Pinochet pressures and maneuvers so the people will not do justice against his cohorts, the torturers and murderers; just as the United States turns a blind eye and "forgets" those details when it comes time to take cases of human rights violations to Geneva, there are others, however, who do not forget and persecute those responsible for so many crimes. For example, a Notimex news dispatch from Asunción says that judge Nelson Alcides Mora will ask for the extradition of dictator Alfredo Stroessner, who is exiled in Brazil, taking into consideration that his chief of police and other persons in his government were sentenced to 25 years in jail. Paraguayan dictator Stroessner was in power for 35 years.

In Nicaragua, after U.S. intervention and Sandino's assassination, Washington guaranteed its domination by placing Somoza in power, a man whose actions in that country we know all about. Somoza's dynasty in Nicaragua lasted 30 years. The United States broke relations with the dictator the same year he was overthrown by the Sandinistas.

In Haiti, after 19 years of intervention and occupation, the interventionist troops sowed the seed of what was to be the sinister Duvalier dynasty.

After the defeat of Trujillo's long tyranny in the Dominican Republic, the United States did everything possible to stop a popularly supported government from coming to power and imposed a Trujillo follower who guaranteed the continuity of their domination.

With the last U.S. intervention in Panama, the United States not only left its own hand-picked man in power, but went so far as to swear him in—so there would be no doubt—at one of its military bases.

The list of crimes would be endless. All of them have been to the United States' advantage: its policy has been based on military and economic superiority.

During all those years, at no time did the U.S. government bother to talk about human rights, or of breaking relations with those governments which had cut themselves off from democracy, and much less of imposing on them an iron-fisted economic blockade. It was an accomplice to all of them and participated in one way or another, directly or indirectly, in all the operations organized to overthrow governments that were elected by the people in the framework of elections imposed by the bourgeoisie itself.

Apart from the common graves where thousands of fighters for social justice lie, the wounds left by our debased sovereignty, and even greater poverty and dependency, we were left with the same political and military structures—under a different guise, of course—to guarantee the continuity of U.S. exploitation, plunder and domination. Thanks to the complicity of domestic bourgeoisies, sustained by Made in USA bayonets, the government of the United States has never permitted a popular government to vindicate and redeem the dispossessed masses.

It would be paradoxical and even ridiculous to have doubts as to the democratic nature of a country which has had more plebiscites of all kinds than any other country in the last 36 years. Millions of persons have supported the Revolution with their physical presence at gigantic rallies and millions of persons have marched through the streets to condemn their enemies' aggressions.

All these facts compel us to find solutions that will force the powerful to respect us as sovereign and independent nations. In our opinion, the only way to achieve this is through Latin American unity.

DANGEROUS SECRETS

I believe in the apostles born in trenches in the fatigue under the singing trees.

—Rafael Quevedo Infante

Social struggles are usually presented using hazy language to hide their true essence, distort reality and disguise the facts and history. Literature giving some light on these struggles is persecuted, forbidden and condemned because it contains what we call "dangerous secrets".

The powerful groups governing the socioeconomic systems we live in share the common denominator of considerable fortunes, and represent the ruling social class. Those people who own only their two arms with which to work constitute another social class: the dispossessed.

The first class, the opulent one, is the owner of all means of production and services, banks, mines, factories, land, insurance. According to Senator Sanders, in the United States this class owns 37% of the wealth, but makes up barely 1% of the population. In worldwide terms, the ruling class constitutes only 20% of the population and owns 87% of all the wealth. In Latin America, among other riches it owns 95% of arable land and makes up only 10% of the population.

In politics there is a universally accepted axiom: whoever has economic power also has political power. This and no other is the reason why the ruling classes in those socioeconomic systems can impose their criteria, distribute wealth in such an unjust manner, dictate their own laws and programs based on the philosophy of plunder, spread their ideology through the communications media they control, create their repressive apparatuses and manage the electoral system guaranteeing continuity in power. They also wield judicial, legislative and executive power and therefore leave no space for the other social classes. They hold virtually absolute power. This is why the U.S. ruling class is opposed to the tendency to increase the number of basic human rights, since this would be tantamount to giving the dispossessed more rights.

However, they need to sell an image of equal rights, fraternity and equality to keep up the appearance of a happy coexistence. With this objective, the magazine *¿Qué es la democracia?* states that:

> When a representative democracy functions according to a constitution that limits government powers and guarantees the fundamental rights of all citizens, such a form of government is a constitutional democracy. In such a society the majority governs and the rights of the minority are protected by law and through the institutionalization of the same.[88]

Nevertheless, independent Senator Bernard Sanders confesses, according to a Notimex press agency dispatch datelined Miami, July 28, 1994:

> Each day it becomes more evident that political decisions, which are part of U.S. consciousness, are made by a small group of people. . . .

> That group's power is consolidated because the big mass media (television, radio, newspapers and magazines) are controlled by the multinationals that "determine what is news and the type of programs we will watch on TV."[89]

In reality, the United States is governed by a plutocracy.

If the dictionary defines plutocracy as government by the wealthy, could a common citizen in that society aspire to have

---

88. Howard Cincotta. Op. cit., 5.
89. "Opina congresista que EE.UU. está en camino de convertirse en oligarquía" (Congressman States U.S. Is On the Way to Becoming an Oligarchy), loc. cit.

a minimum of political power without the backing of a fortune?

Postulates and reality do not always coincide, and that is why the majority of U.S. citizens and of people living in the Third World ask themselves where the rights of four-fifths of the world's population are guaranteed. Neither plutocrats nor oligarchs will be able to resolve with their neoliberal formulas the enormous problems weighing down 80% of our planet's population. They are too busy increasing and defending the fortunes which will keep them in the highest spheres of power.

The U.S. people themselves—according to Sanders—are not sure that their vote can change the country's future and that is why they abstain. In the 1994 legislative elections, 61.3% of the electors abstained and in the last presidential elections, in which Clinton was elected, only 43% voted. If the results are analyzed you will find that the president was elected by approximately one fourth of the U.S. electors. This denies the democratic nature of those elections.

I

No one can fool a people by telling them that their rights are respected when the legal system absolves policemen who have beaten up a citizen, almost killing and disfiguring him; when it is discovered that innocent people have been sentenced to the electric chair; when information on those responsible for crimes committed by persons in the high echelons of power is hidden from them for 100 years; when unjust wars are unleashed and aggressions are carried out against other countries for the sake of egoistic interests; when a man of genius such as Chaplin is expelled and threatened and is accused of being a communist for the sole reason of rightly criticizing the injustice of U.S. society; when another genius, Pablo Picasso, is put on a blacklist; when men and women are discriminated against because of the color of their skin, their gender or social background, as shown by the controversial Proposition 187 that was approved in California; when ethnic minorities are treated as fifth-rate citizens, although the postulates state that their rights are protected by law and through the latter's institutionalization; when the overthrow of governments and the assassination of heads of state elected by popular consensus are ordered.

Among the few concessions that the U.S. government grants to the oppressed classes is the right of all citizens to receive the same protection before the law and to have access to due legal process and a fair trial.

But these postulates didn't work for Rodney King, nor for the Rosenbergs or any of the many other innocent people whose death sentences were carried out. These rights didn't work for the thousands of so-called "excludable" Cubans, or for those who returned after being imprisoned for years for no reason at all, or for those who remain in jail under inhuman conditions and with no legal counsel. Abstract rights and liberties are of no use. If one does not have sufficient human compassion to consider education and health care as human rights, of what use is freedom of expression for the millions of illiterate, marginalized and homeless people in the United States and the Third World if no one listens to them?

II

Today, on the 208th anniversary of the approval of the Constitution of the United States, we read Mr. Sanders' bitter revelations: "Every passing day our economic development resembles more that of any of the so-called developing countries of the Third World. . . ."[90]

Perhaps this is why in his administration's program the current U.S. president promises the people: to eliminate violence in the streets and schools; to help communities to open youth

90. Ibid.

centers; to guarantee that each citizen, independently of his social level, has adequate medical care; to prioritize the fight against AIDS; to guarantee children's safety, education and health care; to do away with drugs in schools; to protect the rights of women in the workplace; and to take forceful measures against violence against women.[91]

While President Clinton is discussing the pursuit of these objectives in Congress, the Cuban people are fighting to maintain these and other achievements. At the same time, they are confronting a economic blockade which is precisely intended to neutralize the progress attained.

While Clinton promises to eliminate violence in the schools and in the streets, the Cuban people are struggling to keep all schools open and for all children to have school supplies, to maintain quality education, to upgrade the teaching staff's qualifications and to avoid—as a consequence of the financial deterioration brought on by the economic blockade—school dropouts. These efforts resulted in a 1993-94 school year with an enrollment of 2,156,569 students and 213,578 teachers, 174,189 of whom were actively employed in the field, for an enviable average of 12.38 students per teacher.

While the U.S. president argues in vain with the power groups in Congress to fulfill his promise of guaranteeing each citizen adequate medical care, independently of their social level, Cuba is struggling at home to maintain the quality of the medical and hospital services offered free of charge to all the country's citizens, and abroad it is trying to find possible ways to circumvent the economic blockade which prevents the entry of medicines and raw materials for their manufacture, equipment, supplies, medical literature, and even life-saving pacemakers.

91. Bill Clinton and Al Gore. *The People Come First*, 38-108.

While the fight against AIDS is just a promise in Clinton's program, Cuba is struggling to maintain the low level of HIV infection (some 1,000 cases) thanks to a vigorous and efficient campaign started many years ago. It is also working to continue giving humane treatment to people suffering from AIDS, and through a multidisciplinary team it cares for and prepares persons with HIV and AIDS for out-patient treatment that will allow them to be reintegrated into society, where they can lead as normal a life as possible in a familiar and loving environment.

If the presence of drugs in schools is a headache for the Democratic president, in Cuba it isn't necessary to waste time or resources to deal with a problem that doesn't exist in the country.

While the worried U.S. president is struggling to keep his promise of protecting women's rights, respect and admiration for this important sector of society is a given in Cuba.

Even the name of Clinton's program, "The People Come First", is more of a reality in Cuba than in the United States.

III

With good reason Cubans think and say that the United States has absolutely nothing to teach them about democracy. They also think that U.S. leaders have no interest whatsoever in having people from other parts of the world know of the Cuban model of democracy.

One of the bourgeois power group's most zealously kept secrets is that the state is a repressive apparatus used to defend the interests of the dominant class. There are daily examples of this: when the masses—irritated and desperate—rush out into the streets in an unequal battle to defend the few rights they need to survive, they are viciously crushed by the repressive state apparatus. The suspension of constitutional guarantees and curfews are additional repressive instruments used every day to neutralize and quench the working class' anger.

The Venezuelan, Dominican, Haitian, Bolivian, Chilean, Central American, in short, the Latin American peoples, as well as the Asian, African and Arab peoples know firsthand about this bourgeois "democratic" attitude.

IV

During bourgeois elections an effort is made to hide from the workers the fact that these elections constitute a hoax and a maneuver by the parties that organize them in complicity with the upper class. It's a very expensive spectacle to ensure the continuity of power in a climate of apparent equity and equality of opportunities. The people's only option in this farce is to use their vote to decide which of the candidates—all of whom are committed to defending the rights of the bourgeoisie—will be the class enemies occupying the top government echelons. Through their vote, the people try to guess who their executioners will be.

The workers' untiring struggle makes it possible for them to sometimes have a candidate sensitive to the interests of the poor within the bourgeois electoral framework. For those cases (or better said, against those cases), the upper class has at its disposal an arsenal of variants. For example, it wasn't convenient for Gaitán in nearby Colombia, or Aquino in the faraway Philippines, to come to power, because they wouldn't defend the ruling minority's interests. Men like Sandino, capable of confronting the U.S. occupation forces to defend national interests, were dangerous. They were all assassinated. It wasn't convenient either for elections to be held in Cuba in 1952, since the Cuban Orthodox Party would have won them; that is why there was a coup d'etat. When a popular leader overcomes all the obstacles set by the bourgeoisie and the United States and is elected, other variants are put to work, such as the one used against Arbenz in Guatemala, or against Allende in Chile; the representatives of the working class who are able to gain power do so for a very short time.

None of these misdeeds occur without the participation of the U.S. government, although in the majority of cases they camouflage their actions, giving them the name of "covert actions". This class struggle's fundamental contradiction lies in the interests of the underdeveloped countries' workers and the interests of the developed countries' plutocracies.

Jacobo Arbenz was overthrown by the CIA when he started carrying out structural changes benefitting his people and thereby affected the interests of U.S. transnationals, specifically the interests of the United Fruit Company.

Salvador Allende, who was elected president by popular suffrage, was prevented from carrying out his government's program by the judicial and legislative powers—both in the hands of the former bourgeois apparatus—and thanks to the major role played by the CIA, which financed and organized the operations that violently ended the government and the life of the intransigent socialist leader.

During the time that the Chilean president was in power, credits from the International Monetary Fund, World Bank and International Development Bank were suspended with the purpose of plunging the country into an economic crisis which would generate popular unrest. However, the Pentagon kept up its aid to and collaboration with the Chilean military during that period and gave them more credits. In conclusion, they weakened the figure who defended the people's interests and strengthened their pawn, Pinochet, a fascist by conviction who after the coup that overthrew Allende immediately gave back to the U.S. transnationals the sectors that were nationalized by the assassinated president.

Juan Bosh, also democratically elected for his positions in favor of the people's interests, had won the hatred of the Dominican upper class and, of course, that of the U.S. State Department: he was overthrown. Balaguer, a Trujillo follower, is to Washington's liking and precisely because of this he has been in power for seven terms without any interference from U.S. administrations.

V

As is clearly seen, this has nothing to do with a local or regional struggle. The bourgeoisie's interests are the same in any part of the world; they identify and interrelate with those of the big U.S. corporations to make up a universal upper class whose command center is run by the developed countries' plutocracies. On the whole, as a class it is not nationalistic; on the contrary, by nature it is reactionary. The only religion they believe in is personal wealth and their favorite ritual is increasing it.

The bourgeoisie in power does not spare methods or conceal its cruelty in repressing the other classes. After Arbenz' overthrow, 150,000 of Guatemala's best sons and daughters were murdered and 52,000 have disappeared.[92] In Pinochet's Chile or the Argentina of military coups, tens of thousands of persons suffered the cruelest tortures and abuses. Similar cases occurred in El Salvador, Honduras, Panama, Nicaragua, Brazil, in the Dominican Republic during the Trujillo period, Batista's Cuba, Pérez Jiménez's and Betancourt's Venezuela, Rojas Pinillas' Colombia, Duvalier's Haiti, and Stroessner's Paraguay, along with many other countries whose bourgeoisies have been able to stay in power on the basis of the inhumane repression of their peoples.

A further example is the social composition of the mercenary brigade with which the United States wanted to give back

92. Juan Dufflar Amel. "Estados Unidos implantó en Guatemala el primer plan neofascista en el continente" (United States Establishes in Guatemala First Neo-fascist Plan in the Continent), in *Trabajadores* newspaper, June 27, 1994, 5.

power to the bourgeoisie overthrown by the Cuban people's struggle. Out of the 1,000 mercenaries, 800 were former owners of property that amounted to 370,077 hectares of land nationalized by the Agrarian Reform Law, 9,666 houses, 70 industries, ten sugar mills, two banks, two newspapers and five mines.

More than 200 of those 800 mercenaries were members of Havana's most exclusive and aristocratic clubs. Of the other 200,135 were ex military men in Batista's army. The remaining 65 were classless people who were in charge of the dirty work—very important people for any self-respecting bourgeoisie—along with torturers, assassins, gamblers, pimps, that is, lumpen elements.[93]

The low moral standards and grim intentions were not concealed. That is why a Miami station broadcast—with the absolute consent of the U.S. authorities—a petition for a three-day license to kill when the counterrevolutionaries were able to get back the control of government in Cuba. This attitude makes clear two important things: that the Cuban government and people's adversary was a resentful bourgeoisie that was using criminal methods to recover its privileges, and that the U.S. government's attitude was unlawful and meant to benefit a small group against the will of an entire people, thus taking an evidently anti-democratic position befitting its class policy.

However, this was not the spirit reigning among the victorious people towards the defeated mercenaries in the failed 1961 Bay of Pigs adventure. The whole world was witness to the respectful and generous treatment given by the Cuban people to the defeated mercenary army. There wasn't a single case of torture, murder or disappearance. Never before had history recorded an attitude such as that of a head of government who respectfully discussed with his adversaries ethical and moral

93. *Playa Girón: derrota del imperialismo* (The Bay of Pigs: A Defeat for Imperialism), vol. 4: 7-8.

questions. No one was humiliated or mistreated, despite the fact that the Cuban state is also the repressive apparatus of the class in power. The main difference is that one of the working class' central philosophies was respect for the integrity and human rights of all persons, and as a matter of principle it could not act in the same way as its adversaries.

According to the postulates of democracy, the minority should submit to the majority. The mercenary invasion demonstrated that the U.S. government was on the side of the minority. The United States hasn't mended its ways; on the contrary, it has maintained this attitude for more than 35 years.

The U.S. government's aid to the minority groups displaced from power in Cuba is not given selflessly. Between 1950 and 1960, the U.S. transnationals took one billion dollars out of Cuba, and they continue to plunder our poor countries through the neoliberal system.

> In interest payments alone [on Latin America's foreign debt], the continent has handed over 360 billion dollars to the developed North in ten years. . . .

> Even the IMF admits that between 1980 and 1987, the nations of the underdeveloped South failed to receive more than 200 billion dollars due to the decreasing prices of their exports. . . . The World Bank reported that all non-petroleum basic products suffered a 20 to 25% decrease in their former prices. Some products, such as fruit juices, had a 50% drop in price.[94]

All that plunder has taken on different forms. Firstly, when our countries were colonies and later, when they were turned into pseudorepublics. Today, they fleece us with neoliberalism, whose fundamental instrument is privatization, that is, selling our national patrimony to power groups, almost always for-

94. Elsa Claro. "Un mundo ancho y ajeno" (A Wide and Foreign World), in *Bohemia* magazine, March 19, 1993, 9-12.

eign. This involves a procedure in which the bourgeoisie accumulates more and more wealth and the workers become poorer and poorer. Meanwhile, our countries become more dependent, more impoverished, losing their sovereignty and identity. Many of these maneuvers are carried out under the guise of representative democracy.

When some secrets stop being secrets, they are usually described as necessary or indispensable evils and defects. For people to be able to accept them, other realities are concealed from them by means of prohibitions. In *¿Qué es la democracia?* it is said: "Democracy cannot guarantee anything on its own. What it offers is the opportunity to be successful and the risk of failure."[95]

In *¿Qué es una economía de mercado?*, the twin sister of the aforementioned magazine, it is stated that:

> People have the freedom to follow the career of their choice but only those who are capable of achieving the basic standards in their chosen employment can remain on the employer's payroll. In competitive markets, firms cannot afford to continue paying employees who are not capable of or do not wish to carry out the tasks for which   they were hired.[96]

In another paragraph it is stated:

> Workers in market economies clearly take on costs and risks if they decide to get an education and additional training. In all truth, some of these investments do not yield interest, because not everyone who goes to a school of higher learning is successful in this or in the job market after graduation.[97]

95. Howard Cincotta. Op. cit., 13.
96. Michael Watts. *¿Qué es una economía de mercado?* (What is a Market Economy?), June 1992, 15.
97. Ibid.

Insecurity, like the sword of Damocles, hangs over the heads of the workers. This diabolical and inhumane philosophy produces millions of unemployed, suicides, streetpeople. In short, it is the negation of the most elemental of human rights. The great amassers of wealth cannot afford to apportion a small part of their fabulous profits to train those who make them rich, and much less provide them with life or health insurance.

When we compare this with the Cuban system, we see that the difference is astronomical. Cuba trains and retrains its workers free of charge. The most important secret behind this system is the one mentioned by an Argentine ABA lawyer to the effect that Cuba was a model of national income distribution, which guarantees innumerable rights for its population.

Perhaps figures can give a clearer picture:

According to the *World Almanac 1994,* Cuba's 1992 GDP showed a per capita income of 1,900 pesos. This is the same as saying that each Cuban received 185 pesos a month or 5.27 pesos a day; equitably distributed this guarantees health care, education, culture, sports, recreation, independence, sovereignty and liberty. This is possible because it is society itself that distributes the country's wealth. The United States has a GDP of 5.610 billion dollars for a per capita income of 22,261 dollars a year. If that income were to be equitably distributed, each citizen would receive 61.83 dollars a day to guarantee—if those fabulous resources would not land in the plutocrats' pockets—all those rights enjoyed by the Cuban people.[98]

If we take the Cuban system as an example, we can define democracy as the policy that on principle is applied by society to equitably distribute the GDP among the nation's citizens.

Therefore we can conclude that the biggest crime, the unforgivable sin committed by Cuba, consists in having permanently done away with the myth about socialism before the world and demonstrating that it means—both in theory and in prac-

98. *World Almanac 1994,* pp. 562-563.

tice—true democracy, according to the postulates proclaimed by capitalism's theoreticians.

VI

The value of these sociological discoveries lies in the fact that many years before Fidel Castro's ascent to power, the developed countries' dominant classes set their minds—through a systematic, costly and well-mounted campaign—on devaluing and discrediting the word socialism. For this they used the word democracy as a counterpoint to socialism, turning them into antonyms. To say socialism was to say heresy, crime, treason; it was identified as the antithesis of the American dream.

To achieve this rejection of socialism they resorted to absurd and puerile stories: they presented the socialist state as a monster that deprived parents of authority over their children. They said that in such societies women were treated as collective property, as were material goods like houses, automobiles, toothbrushes; in other words, there wasn't the slightest vestige of individuality. When they wanted to get rid of people they accused them of being socialist—it didn't matter if they weren't—and expelled them from the country, persecuted them, murdered them or made them disappear. They also proscribed materialist philosophy and political economy.

Strange as it may seem, today, on the threshold of the 21st century, this story hasn't come to an end: U.S. citizens cannot enjoy the right of freedom to travel, since they are forbidden from traveling to Cuba; Miami counterrevolutionary radio stations, subsidized by the government of the United States, violate all the international agreements related to radiophonic space and continue disseminating the most incredible slander against Cuba. They use 17 radio stations and broadcast 1, 700 hours of diatribe monthly.

Therefore, it is easy to understand why some U.S. presidents who have promising programs, drawn up in all good faith, are not able to make them come true. Such is the case with President Clinton's health care program. He couldn't convince the power groups in Congress, those who represent Wall Street's interests. Since they are not inclined to have "democratic weaknesses" in detriment to their personal fortunes, to benefit the poor sectors, they distributed 300 million dollars among the decision-making levels to postpone until next year the urgent needs of U.S. workers. This is the reason for Clinton's bitter lament when he stated that their decision had left all the powerful interests in possession of everything they already had.[99]

To whom was Clinton referring? It's worthwhile quoting two paragraphs that clearly explain this:

> Clinton's project establishes in some parts that companies should pay the largest share of the aforementioned insurance for its staff. It also extends the benefits for senior citizens, the unemployed and other persons, as well as establishing price controls in the field of medical care.

> The majority of the U.S. people back the general objectives of the government's intentions, but...the country's most important employers organization, the Business Round Table, was openly against them. . . .[100]

In daily practice, the bourgeoisie has once again—because of selfishness and greed—come out against the elemental rights of the working class.

VII

Another of the secrets that the bourgeoisie has zealously concealed is the main source of its wealth. Human labor is highly productive, and with the use of scientific and technical

99. Nicanor León Cotayo. "¿Quién manda en los Estados Unidos?" (Who's in Charge in the United States?), in *Granma* daily, July 23, 1994, 5.
100. Ibid.

advances it brings in big dividends, it is extremely profitable. People produce more riches than they receive in salaries and benefits; therefore, the difference goes into the bourgeoisie's coffers.

When one finds out about the huge fortunes in the hands of the powerful and their insatiable appetites for indefinitely increasing them, one can understand why they eagerly conceal the fact that an authentic democracy can only exist through radical structural changes, because it is impossible to reconcile their interests, rights, needs and aspirations with those of the workers. Democracy cannot exist where there is no equality of rights and opportunities.

And neither can we qualify as democratic a system that employs an economic blockade, aggressions, slander, interventions and dirty wars against another system that is more humane, more just, more equitable. These are the moral standards of so-called U.S. democracy. It can't teach anything to anyone, not even to the U.S. people themselves.

It was precisely during the unjust war unleashed by the United States against the Vietnamese people that the first symptoms of moral cracks in U.S. ideals began to appear. The soldiers started to avoid being drafted or deserted; they began to realize that in that war they were defending the plutocratic minority's narrow-minded interests. It is thus that the cracks began to appear in the empire's moral standards, a clear sign of what will be the irremediable collapse of its unjust system.

As a result, some people in the United States are channeling their desire for social justice into activities of solidarity with other peoples. In Cuba's case, the economic blockade has led to a movement encompassing a heterogeneous range of people with differing religious beliefs and political views, in the United States and elsewhere. People began to realize that the economic blockade on Cuba is so unjust, immoral and illegal that it goes beyond political considerations to become an ethical and humane issue. This is the reason why men and women worldwide are calling for the elimination of the economic blockade.

The comparison of the Cuban reality with that of the Third World countries has brought out in the open the fundamental contradiction in the Cuba-U.S. conflict. The underdeveloped countries have become aware that the Cuban people's struggle is the same as that being carried out by them and that the common enemy is in the wealthy metropoli.

The Latin American countries have access to enough data to be able to state that the developed countries, in complicity with the power groups that rule them, have extracted raw materials at far below their real cost; they have manipulated the economy and have artificially devalued their currencies to benefit their interests; they have made them the victims of unequal trade; and in exchange have left underdevelopment, poverty, illiteracy, unemployment, a secular backwardness.

Currently, economists calculate that in one year the developed countries extract more riches from Latin America than the Spanish colonialists did in 300 years. With this example of plunder, anyone can come to the conclusion that in today's world the obsolete and worn-out system of bourgeois democracy does not have the solution for the grave problems faced by humanity. The Third World will not be able to do away with their degrading underdevelopment and social inequality with the type of democracy proposed by the United States.

The magazine *¿Qué es la democracia?* recognizes that "economic questions [have become] the main force that divides— and defines—the political spectrum of 'the left and the right', as it is known today."[101]

The left has always stated that the key, the essence of the struggle and of the division of society into social classes is due to economic factors. To define the nature of a system it should suffice to determine if the country's riches are in the hands of

101. Howard Cincotta. Op. cit., 29.

the people or in the hands of a privileged few, that is, in private hands.

According to the aforementioned magazine:

> Democracy does not imply a certain economic doctrine. The democratic governments have accepted on an equal footing the most dedicated socialists and those who favor the free market...those who propose democracy usually consider economic freedom as a key element in every democratic society.[102]

This is not a paradox or a contradiction. When they accept socialists and then persecute them it is a question of double standards. They have ruined our countries precisely in the name of that economic freedom. In this way they invested 20 billion dollars in the ill-fated Alliance for Progress and now we have a debt of 500 billion dollars which provoked a socioeconomic situation far worse than the one we had before they gave us that "aid". It is in the name of that economic freedom that they plague our peoples with hunger and poverty, as foreseen by Simón Bolívar.

We can then come to the conclusion that a socioeconomic system is good for the workers if the United States attacks and combats it, but if it defends and praises it, then it is very bad for them.

VIII

The secrets we have revealed here are highly dangerous. They bring to light the capitalist system's vulnerable points. The clandestine common graves disseminated throughout all of the Third World hold the remains of many of those who knew these secrets and struggled to better the living standards

102. Ibid.

of their peoples. Those who make up the long lists of disappeared were persons who, in their majority, were up to date on these secrets. Che Guevara, Salvador Allende, Fabricio Ojeda, Jorge E. Gaitán, Carlos Fonseca, Augusto C. Sandino, Francisco Caamaño and many others were assassinated because they knew these secrets and fought for their peoples.

HUMAN RIGHTS

Respect for the rights of others is peace.
—Benito Juárez

If everyone were to follow the wise philosophy of this worthy Mexican patriot, and its fulfillment were an indispensable prerequisite for winning the Nobel Peace Prize, in all justice this prize should go to Cuba. No country has struggled so much in recent years for the respect of its rights and those of others.

Unfortunately, for the United States there is no right other than that of a small group of that country's ruling hierarchy. They neither respect nor recognize anyone else's rights and impose—as a divine right—the law of the strongest on the rest of the world. There is no country in which they haven't intervened in one way or another. As can be seen, for U.S. hegemony there are no moral principles, international law, charters or agreements that merit respect. The law of the strongest—which has no relation to civilization or democracy—is the only law applied by U.S. leaders, and to this end they have resorted to manipulating other countries at the United Nations, a strategy used to disguise the unilateral character of their aggressions.

This has obliged the Cuban people to arm themselves in word and deed. Martí believed that a just principle at the bottom of a cave was worth more than an army. This is very true; however, apart from ideas, Cubans have created the conditions to be an army of 11 million inhabitants ready to fight back against any aggression. Thanks to this determination, among other factors, the war that Cubans have had to endure for many years has been one without bombs.

Among the weapons used by the United States against Cuba during all these years are the repeated accusations of hypothetical violations of human rights.

After getting to know Cuba's socioeconomic system, it would be ridiculous to waste time refuting such lies, but it would be useful to verify the absolute hypocrisy of the prosecutors.

In March 1994, Cuba presented before the national and foreign press a secret document sent by the U.S. Interests Section in Havana (USINT) to the State Department in Washington, with a copy for that country's Immigration and Naturalization Service (INS). Here are a few paragraphs from the document:

Update on the Cuban Refugee Program[103]

I. OVERVIEW

The processing of refugee applicants continues to show weak cases. Most people apply more because of the deteriorating economic situation than a real fear of persecution. Cases presented by human rights activists prove particularly difficult for USINT officers and INS members. Although we have tried hard to work with those human rights organizations on which we exert greater control to identify activists truly persecuted by the government, human rights cases represent the weakest category of the refugee program. . . .

Common allegations of fraudulent applications by activists and of the sale of testimonials by human rights leaders have continued in recent months. Due to the lack of verifiable documentary evidence, as a rule USINT officers and INS members have regarded human rights cases as the most susceptible to fraud.

II. ASSESSMENT

The decrease in the number of political prisoners led the State Department and the INS three years ago to work together in expanding the categories for processing in the Cuban Refugee Program. . . .

During later INS visits, USINT made a deliberate effort to include cases from all of the categories. . . .

Although USINT has tried to cover cases in line with the processing criteria, it has nonetheless preserved its flexibility to present cases

103. "Top Secret", in *Granma International,* March 16, 1994, 11, 4.

that may fall short in some areas but represent an interest to US.

A deteriorating Cuban economy has provided incentive for new economic migrants to seek the refugee program. . . .

It is brazenly acknowledged now by some of the reintegrated ex-political prisoners that they apply for refugee status as a means to escape the deteriorating economic situation and not because of a current fear of persecution or harassment. . . .

Regrettably, the general quality of many of the applications is poor. . . . Most ex-political prisoners played lesser roles in counterrevolutionary groups, accepted political reeducation in order to have their sentences reduced, and later abandoned political activity to reintegrate into Cuban society. . . .

We have recorded an increase in the number of human rights cases since 1992. However, this increase did not stem from a higher level of human rights activity. The majority of cases rarely contain any demonstrable evidence of persecution and frequently give only minimal, hardly credible, evidence of participation in human rights activities.

The testimonials of human rights leaders generally carry vague descriptions of human rights activity, such as the moral support of family members of political prisoners. . . .

On the other hand, almost none of the cases show proof of house searches, interrogations, detention or arrest. The activists usually claim persecution by State Security, but they rarely can provide properly documented evidence of it. In some instances the applicant claims to have been subject to harassment without arrest. . . .

The general trend has been one of lack of evidence to prove that the person is actually an activist, which leaves the category open for virtually everyone. Young men caught in illegal exit attempts since the economic downturn in 1989 (collapse of the socialist bloc) have tended to submit applications as human rights activists. Human rights leaders have told USINT officers that they know that most of their members joined only to take advantage of the refugee program. . . .

In cases where the activist's supporting evidence is weak, but commitment to US is otherwise clear, prescreening officers have given the applicant the benefit of the doubt.

The leader of one group said that several people left his organization when they knew that it does not give testimonials to members. . . .

The latest INS visits have witnesses repeated incidences of fraud and allegations of fraud by human rights activists. USINT has attempted to address the problem through a revision of internal procedures to identify strong human rights cases. . . .

To our regret, not even these steps have prevented allegations of fraud and bitter recriminations among top human rights leaders. . . .

Out of the 225 cases presented by USINT to INS during its December visit, 47 claimed involvement in human rights activity. . . .

Of all 47 human rights cases, only one claimed a total of more than 30 days detention over the last five years for human rights activity, and even he could not provide evidence of the detentions. . . . Most activists gave only vague descriptions of their involvement in human rights groups. And only 19 were finally approved. . . .

The overall refusal rate for the December visit as a result was 22 percent. This rate, although significantly higher than in past INS visits, has on the sideline the advantage of hopefully resulting in a higher level of activity by the groups.

CONSIDERATIONS

In the face of a general decline in the quality of the cases, including those involving ex-political prisoners, USINT will need to work harder in identifying the best cases. With a view to help in this effort, it will introduce additional changes in the processing of cases.

The problems encountered in the processing of the bulk of the human rights cases point to the need for USINT to continue its close work with the INS to select strong cases.

However, the USINT will maintain the flexibility to present cases that may not meet all of the criteria but that given their nature may prove useful for US interests.

Given CIA's expressed interests in the subject of human rights, and its greater involvement with and better knowledge of the different groups, we suggest a closer cooperation with USINT in line with our common goals.

Joseph Sullivan

This report illustrates—better than any Cuban denunciation—the United States' irreverent hoax on the international community each time it takes this issue to Geneva. With this proof of the violation of every document ever written so that the rights of states be respected, it is not necessary for anyone to accuse the United States. They have unmasked and accused themselves.

Mr. Sullivan leaves no room for doubt that the immense majority of those applying for a visa to emigrate to the United States do so for strictly economic reasons, as a consequence of the deteriorating conditions brought on by the commercial, economic and financial blockade imposed on Cuba for 35 years.

The document makes it clear that these counterrevolutionary groups are not representative, and thus the idea of achieving a corrosive process from the bottom up to make the people ungovernable has become utopic.

Moreover, it reveals the weakness of the arguments used concerning so-called violations of human rights and political persecution. It also recognizes the base moral standards of the leaders of those groups, who accuse each other of selling fraudulent testimonials for financial gain.

This report also bears witness to the lack of harassment and persecution on the part of the Cuban government towards those who proclaim such lies. It is worth clarifying that the majority of the crimes committed by members of these groups are common ones, of the type persecuted and condemned in any country in the world, although the report places them among counterrevolutionaries who are truly persecuted by the government.

The document touches only briefly upon the existence of a penitentiary system which respects human beings and gives them the opportunity to become reeducated and reintegrated into society.

The mere existence of a refugee program offering special privileges and distinguishing Cubans from people of other nationalities in itself stimulates the counterrevolutionary groups. It politicizes immigration and distorts its economic character, so as to conceal the causes for it, which are the same as those for people of other nationalities wishing to emigrate to the United States.

The report recognizes that there is a close and direct relationship between the decreasing number of political prisoners and that of common prisoners.

The document further confirms the denunciations Cuba has been making for many years when it recognizes the CIA's interest in the subject of human rights.

Moreover, they promise to prioritize and be flexible in those cases that could be of use to U.S. interests.

The document also reveals the lack of unity, serious motivations and popular support of these human rights groups that are manipulated from abroad. Throughout these 35 years of confrontations, not one of these groups has presented the Cuban people with a program offering useful alternatives. There can be no so-called political confrontation because these groups don't have a political program, which demonstrates that what actually exists is a conflict between the Revolution and the counterrevolution. This is the reason why Cubans say there are not political prisoners in their country, but rather counterrevolutionary prisoners. Their activities against Cuba benefit only the interests of the United States, so these annexationists basically play the role of vulgar mercenaries.

It seems incredible that the United States can level accusations of human rights violations against a country which has achieved the most significant social successes in the Third World and at the same time shelter the criminals who blew up a passenger plane and who pursued, harassed and machine-gunned the *Herman,* a ship carrying a Cuban crew, in international waters.

During these 36 years, the counterrevolutionary groups—in complicity with the U.S. government, which has trained, organized, financed, encouraged and sometimes even transported them to Cuban shores—have committed thousands of serious crimes. These groups have consistently violated the right of a people to build their own future.

The tactics of this minority sector are no different from the tactics used by the United States. They both advocate, among other things, a multiparty system in Cuba and the physical elimination of Fidel Castro. They long for a market economy and the application of the unsuccessful neoliberal model. They utilize methods aimed at depreciating the Cuban people's virtues and principles, attacking their roots, their history, their cultural identity.

The flagrant violation of the Cuban people's human rights has brought with it many innocent victims. This is why it is paradoxical that some Cubans calling themselves patriots support those who attack their country, simply because they disagree on certain non-crucial matters. And this is even more so when we know that a minimum of 80% of the major objective problems—mainly economic—that the country is facing are a direct result of the United States' brutal and illegal state of siege and relentless persecution. These self-described patriots obviously haven't understood that the fundamental contradiction lies between the interests of their people and the interests of the aggressor. Or could it be that their purported identity as patriots is nothing more than a disguise to hide their true identity as annexationists, opportunists, or simply crackpots?

Even the most ignorant person understands that in the case of Cuba, the priority lies in resolving the contradiction between the interests of a sovereign and independent country and the annexationist pretensions of the United States. Homeland signifies the endurance of dignity, sovereignty, independence and freedom; without it, everything is lost. This is true for any country.

DEMOCRATIC ELECTIONS

*Article 69. The National Assembly of People's Power
is the supreme body of state power and represents
and expresses the sovereign will of all the people.*
—Constitution of the Republic of Cuba

The most powerful mass media in the history of humanity have used the most virulent and rancorous terms to spread slander against Cuba throughout the world. They have been so successful that whoever hears anything about the holding of elections in Cuba is astonished. No one believes in the validity of elections that stray from the corrupt mechanisms which for many years have been inculcated in us as the only valid ones, and much less if the carnival-like confrontations between two or more parties fiercely contending for power are excluded. Democratic elections with only one party?!

In Venezuela, 48 political parties participate in the elections. So many different tendencies and not a single one with the purpose of working on behalf of the nation! This reality demonstrates the impossibility of drawing up a development strategy and improving the standard of living of our people. When we participate in this farce we make fools of ourselves, while those who wield the real power, economic power, observe with glee the spectacle they have set up to entertain us, leading us to believe that this is the only democratic procedure.

During election time in the United States we are witness to the confrontation between powerful groups, capable of wasting millions of dollars simply for the sake of maintaining power in the hands of the Wall Street chieftains, who are impervious to their people's calamities.

Cuba has demonstrated that it is not necessary to fragment the country to hold truly democratic elections in the interest of the nation.

The Cuban electoral process commences with the election of a delegate in each of the electoral districts that every municipality is divided into. The electors are the ones who propose candidates at meetings held for this purpose. The election of a delegate is carried out via the direct and secret vote of those electors who reside in that district. The elected delegates make up the Municipal Assembly of People's Power.

For the election of delegates to the provincial assemblies and of deputies to the National Assembly of People's Power, national, provincial and municipal candidacy commissions are created to elaborate and present the draft candidacy. These commissions are made up of representatives of the Central Organization of Cuban Trade Unions (which presides it), the Committees for the Defense of the Revolution, the Federation of Cuban Women, the National Association of Small Farmers, the Federation of University Students and the Federation of Students in Intermediate Education.

These commissions will take into account that up to 50% of the candidates are district delegates. The rest may be outstanding citizens in the different spheres of national life.

The propositions for pre-candidates to delegates to the provincial assemblies and deputies to the National Assembly of People's Power are elaborated and then presented to the municipal assemblies for their consideration and approval. The delegates to the provincial assemblies of People's Power and the deputies are elected via the population's direct and secret vote.[104]

It is necessary to emphasize that neither the Communist Party nor the Young Communist League nominate candidates, which makes it possible for any citizen, worker, student, farmer, employee, soldier or housewife to be nominated without being a member of the Party or the League or being a wealthy person.

104. For more information see "Law No. 72. Electoral Law" in the *Gaceta Oficial de la República de Cuba,* November 2, 1992, 51-66.

Their personal background, human qualities, patriotism, and integrity are sufficient to be elected. This is the secret behind the fact that in the last Cuban elections 98% of the eligible population participated. The explanation is obvious: the Cuban people know that their vote can determine the destiny of the nation, unlike the U.S. people, according to Sanders.

To be elected to any of the bodies of power does not represent a privilege in Cuba, on the contrary, it represents more responsibility, with no remuneration. The delegates carry out their duties after work hours, except the professional cadre who receive the same salary as they received in their former workplace.

Delegates to the municipal assemblies must render accounts to their electors at meetings held every six months, although they may be convened at any time by the delegate or by the electors. In this way, the Cuban people guarantee that those who hold a position of power do so out of disinterested love for the people, not to derive material benefits.

These almost 20-year-old mechanisms have been continuously refined and perfected over the years in that they are deeply rooted in praxis.

The people are the protagonists in the Cuban electoral system, not simply spectators. They participate in the solution of society's problems and contribute to the nation's development. This system makes it possible for common people to play an important role. They discuss, analyze, amend the guiding programs for their lives. There are many examples: the Family Code, the Constitution of the Republic of Cuba, the Penal Code and the workers' parliaments that discussed the documents on the financial reorganization of the economy.

Men and women, workers, pensioners, the military, students, all meet within their organizations as a prolongation of the National Assembly in the search for solutions to the country's serious problems. In all truth, this process is worthy of being studied in depth, not only for its originality but also for its results. The achievements of the Cuban electoral system constitute an appreciable contribution.

If we take into account that the Cuban people have the possibility of defending their achievements with weapon in hand, through the Territorial Troop Militia (MTT), the reserves, or General Military Service, where men and women periodically prepare to defend the nation if necessary, we must admit that all the state powers are in the hands of the people.

However, the situation of other countries in the hemisphere is different. There was a high level of abstentionism in the most recent elections in the region's countries (see Table No. 11 at the end of this chapter), despite the enormous campaigns unleashed by the media to counteract this. The current Venezuelan president was elected by 13-14% of the votes; in Guatemala, 80% of the electors stayed at home. In President Clinton's election, the official figures showed there was a 46% abstention rate. A few months before, Senator Bernard Sanders had calculated there would be a 66% rate of abstentionism and attributed this to the fact that U.S. citizens do not believe their vote can change things.

During the last legislative elections in the United States, the struggle between Republican oil millionaire Michael Huffington and Democrat Dianne Feinstein (wife of a banker) for an electoral seat resulted in the spending of 36 million dollars, of which the Republican—with a personal fortune estimated at 75 million dollars—spent more than 24 million from his own pocket.

In 1992, 504 million dollars were spent in the United States for the election of the 435 members of the House of Representatives and a third of its 100 senators.

It must be pointed out that not one single cent is invested in the Cuban elections for this type of campaigning and propaganda. The photographs and biographies of the candidates, as well as informal, simple and austere meetings with their electors is sufficient for them.

In the magazine *¿Qué es la democracia?*, U.S. ideologues have clearly explained what for them are the pillars of democracy:

- Sovereignty of the people.
- Government based on the consent of the governed.
- Government for the majority.
- Rights for the minority.
- Guarantee of basic human rights.
- Free and just elections.
- Equality before the law.
- Due legal process.
- Constitutional limits to government.
- Social, economic and political pluralism.
- Values of tolerance, pragmatism, cooperation and consensus. [105]

When analyzing the aforementioned we come to the conclusion that these pillars of democracy are still an unfulfilled aspiration in the United States.

105. Howard Cincotta. Op. cit., 6.

Table 12
Results of Last Elections by Country
(1989 a 1992)

Country	Date	Ruling party	Voters[*] (%)	Abstentionism[**] (%)
Argentina	May 1989	Justicialista	44,6	-
Bolivia	1989	MIR-ADN	41,6	26,3
Brazil	Dec 1989	PRN	42,7	19,3
Chile	Dec 1989	Demócrata-Cristiano	55,2	29,4
Colombia	Mar 1990	Liberal	48,0	58,0
Costa Rica	Feb 1990	Unidad Socialista Cristiana	50,2	18,2
Ecuador	May 1992	PUR	28,0	14,0
El Salvador	Mar 1989	ARENA	44,3	9,0
Guatemala	Jan 1991	Movimiento Acción Solidaria	67,0	55,0[****]

			*	**
Honduras	Nov 1989	Nacional	52,0	23,2
Mexico	Jul 1988	PRI	50,3	49,6
Nicaragua	Feb 1990	UNO	54,7	12,5
Paraguay	May 1989	Colorado	68,0	-
Peru	Jun 1990	Cambio 90	56,5	17,0
Puerto Rico	Nov 1992	Nuevo Progresista	50,0	17,0
United States	Nov 1992	Democratic	43,0	46,0****
Uruguay	Nov 1989	Nacional	38,9	-

Source: "Les salió el tiro por la culata" (It Backfired on Them), in *Juventud Rebelde* weekly, Havana, February 28, 1993.

* Percentage of votes in relation to valid votes.

** Possible electors who did not vote.

*** In the July 1994 partial elections, 20% voted and 80% abstained.

**** During the 1994 partial elections, 38% voted and 61% abstained.

RELIGION

He who betrays the poor betrays Christ.

—Fidel Castro

Cuba's unquestionable socioeconomic achievements have had a notable influence in the world, particularly in the underdeveloped countries and especially among Latin America's religious communities. For their part, these communities have influenced their denomination's hierarchy, bringing about reconsiderations and reformulations of core sociological and philosophical importance. An example of this is the interrelation between the Cuban process, Liberation Theology and the 2nd Vatican Council, where there has been favorable feedback. As a result of this, a Latin American theology has emerged to replace the one imported from the Old World.

Brazilian theologian Frei Betto is convinced that "there isn't any similarity between the God in whom the Latin American workers and farmers and I believe—and the god of Reagan. . . ."[106] The same may be applied to Bush, Nixon, Truman, the Kings of Spain who got rich from the slave trade from Africa to America, or the gang of dictators supported or imposed by the United States in our continent. Evidently, the God of the poor masses of the Third World or the developed countries cannot be the same in which Kennedy believed in when he launched the Bay of Pigs invasion or Bush with his merciless attacks against Iraq.

The most objective way to approach the structuring of ideas on religion is precisely by calling on those who have direct knowledge of our realities and who struggle for the well-being

106. Frei Betto, *Fidel & Religion, Conversations with Frei Betto,* Ocean Press publishers, 184.

of their peoples, to whom they are closely linked although they may depart from philosophical concepts which have always been considered antagonistic. All of them are convinced that Latin America is not divided into believers and nonbelievers, but rather into exploited and exploiters. They are conscious, moreover, that our peoples' struggle is not the cause but the consequence of the inhuman exploitation and the terrible social injustice imposed on the poor by a class having an insatiable appetite for riches.

With or without God, the Cuban system doesn't ask the workers if they believe or not to provide them with education, medical care, social services, etc. Human beings are measured by their human, patriotic, ethical, moral and civic values. Thus we are faced with a government that, in pursuit of important common goals, benefits the great majority, the nation, where believers and nonbelievers live in harmony.

The Constitution of the Republic of Cuba stipulates that: "Discrimination because of race, skin color, gender, national origin, religious beliefs and any other form of discrimination harmful to human dignity is forbidden and will be punished by law."[107]

The above is possible because when you work honestly and seriously for the well-being of the people, it is not important whether they believe or don't believe in God. This is reflected in the prologue written by Cuban Minister of Culture Armando Hart to the book *Fidel & Religion,* by Frei Betto:

> A practicing Catholic with deep Christian faith and a communist leader well known for his firm position of principles held an extensive dialogue, and, when the exchange was over, each felt surer of his own convictions and more interested in establishing closer, deeper relations in the practical political struggle. Moreover, each had based his arguments—and this may be the most inter-

---

107. *Constitution of the Republic of Cuba,* loc. cit.

esting aspect for researchers—on the original sources of Christianity and Marxism. Neither of them has ceded at all in his principles, and each understands the other deeply on such important topics as morality, contemporary economic and political problems, and the need for Christians and Communists to unite in the struggle for a better world. . . .

It is a proposition with a solid moral, political and social basis. This, in itself, is a tremendous achievement in the history of human thought. The ethical-moral note appears in these lines to bear the human feeling that unites fight

It wasn't always easy to understand that all those who are struggling in favor of social justice, irregardless of their religious beliefs, hold common points of view. And it was even more difficult because powerful forces worked untiringly to hinder this unity. Reverend Raúl Suárez, a Baptist pastor who heads the Martin Luther King Jr. Memorial Center in Havana and is a deputy to the National Assembly of People's Power, pointed out in an interview he granted to me:

At present old antagonisms have been overcome, both sides have overcome dogmatic schemata, religious schemata influenced by ideas of the time of Pope Pius XII which pictured Marxists as intrinsically bad people and Marxism as a perverse phenomenon. On the other hand, there were Marxists who thought that Christians were people who had serious ideological limitations, that they were reactionaries, counterrevolutionaries, retrogrades.[109]

108. Frei Betto. Op. cit., 3-4.
109. Raúl Suárez. Author's interview with Reverend Rául Suárez, head of the Martin Luther King Jr. Center and deputy to the National Assembly of People's Power, January 1995.

The Cuban reverend and deputy informed us that in his country there are 56 legally registered religious denominations and that the state and church are separate entities, which in no way negatively affects the continuity of religious practices, guaranteed by 12 seminaries for pastoral training.

Fidel Castro confirms the existence of flexibility among believers and atheists in his country: "Some years ago we had difficulties with the Catholic Church but they were solved, and all the problems that existed at a given moment disappeared."[110] He recognizes further on that "There are many doctrinaire Marxists. I think that being doctrinaire on this matter complicates the issue."[111]

Christians believe this position is genuine and constructive. Therefore, the Cuban government receives ever greater support from the continent's Christians, who at the General Assembly of the Latin American Council of Churches (CLAI), held in Concepción, Chile on January 1995, approved a resolution in favor of the lifting of the U.S. economic blockade, described by them as unjust and anti-Christian.

If in 1959, when the rebels took power in Cuba, the religious stance, above all in the Catholic hierarchy, had been more in line with the interests of the people, which is the case today in Cuba and in other countries, all the disagreeable friction which provoked a distancing between the Church hierarchy and the state in the early years would have been avoided.

It was evident for any observer that the changes being made on the island by the new government widely satisfied the needs of the great dispossessed majority. Opposing a government that was placing so many social gains in the hands of the poor signified—and it was thus understood by the vast majority of the Cuban people—the adoption of an openly antipopular position. And many people asked themselves: Is that a Christian position?

110. Frei Betto. Op. cit., 174.
111. Ibid, 15.

The most recalcitrant elements of the defeated ruling class held important positions in the religious hierarchy, especially the Catholic Church. That elite was an ally and accomplice of the tyranny that had unconstitutionally usurped power through a coup d'etat, which explains their rejection of the revolutionary changes. It's not by chance that in a matter of weeks, of months, the new political program gained 95% of the people's support. Proof of this is the fact that the less than 3,000 armed men who came down from the Sierra Maestra in 1959 were transformed into millions of men and women who in April 1961 took up arms to defend their achievements when the United States launched a mercenary invasion through the swamplands of the Zapata Peninsula. The profound changes made by the new government were behind the Cuban people's willingness to endure a holocaust, if necessary, throughout the terrible hours lived by humanity during the October 1962 Missile Crisis.

Meanwhile, the reactionary clergy closed ranks on the side of the opulent and defeated minority, and willingly consented to being the United States' spearhead in its conspiratorial maneuvers to defeat the revolutionary government. The alliance of the reactionary clergy with the Cuban people's historical enemy served to aggravate popular rejection of religious people.

Right from the start it was clear that the fundamental contradiction wasn't between the people and the government, not even between Christians and the government, which is reflected in the Cuban leader's words: "There are still some doctrinaires around, and it's not easy for us, but our relations with the Church are gradually improving. . . ."[112]

Further on Fidel said:

> There was a time when the political confrontation became really fierce, and because of the militant political

112. Ibid, 16.

attitude taken by some priests—especially the Spanish ones—we requested that they be withdrawn from our country, and we revoked their authorization to remain here . . . ., that was the measure that was taken. However, we authorized other priests to come to Cuba and replace the ones who were asked to leave.[113]

Later on Fidel points out that this was the only measure taken and only on this one occasion.

As a curious footnote, I could add that three priests were among those organized, financed and trained by the CIA for the mercenary invasion of the Bay of Pigs.

In Cuba we can find a Baptist pastor who is not a Marxist or a member of the Communist Party but who forms part of the highest body of power as a deputy to the National Assembly of People's Power. This is not an isolated case: there are other religious people who are not Party members but form part of government bodies, due to the existing democratic mechanisms permitting their election.

Reverend Suárez explains it this way: "In the political organization system existing in Cuba, the Party does not propose or elect. This function strictly concerns the people, the residents who make up the electoral districts and their mass organizations."[114]

The Christian deputy tells us that his candidacy stemmed from a proposition made by the workers. Before accepting, he carried out three consultations. The first was with his conscience, before God, to decide if representing the people in this capacity had a biblical, spiritual, theological, pastoral and Christian foundation, "given the fact that I am not a traditional politician but a pastor with a Christian identity at the service of my people"[115]; the second consultation was with the Church and

113. Ibid, 159.
114. Raúl Suárez. Author's interview. . . . Op. cit.
115. Ibid.

the third with the people who have been his neighbors for the past 25 years. The three replies were affirmative. He finds there are no contradictions in being both a parliamentarian and a minister of God in his country. He was elected with 94% of the votes, through an electoral process that he considers to be authentic and carried out in a very serious manner. Its legitimacy is backed by mass participation in the elections.

In past years, Church representatives—Camilo Torres, Father Sardiñas, Ernesto Cardenal—have held the same ideals as those who have struggled politically for structural changes in our America and have shared with the poor the weight of the rural or urban campaigns.

Reverend Suárez believes that this phenomenon is due to the Christian tradition's urgent ethical and prophetic demands, to the biblical foundations of its faith and inspiration, and to the Christian behavior of each one of us. Moreover, he believes these changes are a consequence of the extreme poverty which generates high mortality rates, a low life expectancy, unemployment, illiteracy, poor health and homelessness for millions of people in the Third World. For him, being a Christian and having a pastoral vocation means choosing the option of being with his people. Paraphrasing Camilo Torres, he tells us that the duty of every Christian is to make revolution, and adds that as shown by the Cuban experience, closely linked to the Latin American and Caribbean context, this is the only way of putting into practice the precept of loving your neighbor. This is precisely what the Cuban process has been doing from its beginnings, and closely echoes the teachings of Jesus Christ: giving food to the hungry, water to the thirsty, clothes to the naked, shelter to the destitute, caring for the sick, the widowed, the prisoners. "I choose the people," says the reverend, "which means having a commitment to change the conditions in which millions of people live."[116] And he ends by saying that he finds

116. Ibid.

no contradiction between this position and his Christian faith.

The impact of Cuba's achievements contributed to growing awareness in religious circles, among others.

Undoubtedly, mutual influences and the changes derived from this process contributed to better relations between the Vatican and the Cuban state. Reverend Suárez talks about this: "Relations with the Vatican date back to before the triumph of the Revolution, and they were never broken after 1959. An example of the current state of relations are the cordial and harmonious talks with Cardinal Etchegaray, who recently visited Cuba."[117]

He also made reference to Cuban Foreign Minister Roberto Robaina's visit to the Holy See and recalled the Pope's concern over the need for the normalization of relations with the United States and the lifting of the economic blockade. He also referred to the fact that Cuban nuns have repeatedly voiced their position against the economic blockade and the Torricelli Act.

With these antecedents it is easy to understand that in all parts of the world—especially in the Americas—believers and nonbelievers have generated a movement of solidarity with Cuba as strong as the one taking place in recent times, in the same measure as the inhuman economic blockade is being tightened. This massive and active movement has even conditioned the attitude of many governments as to their stance on Cuba. In the United States, sympathy for the Cuban process has taken the interesting form of civil disobedience, a traditional method of struggle in some religious organizations such as that of Martin Luther King, in which there is not only opposition to the illegal economic blockade but also to the unconstitutional decree which forbids U.S. citizens from traveling to Cuba.

Pastors for Peace is a movement made up of religious activists representing various denominations. As Christians, they spread their message by providing information on the struc-

117. Ibid.

tural changes taking place in Cuba, and tour hundreds of cities collecting aid to help alleviate the hardships brought on by the economic blockade.

In 1988, while in Nicaragua, Reverend Suárez invited U.S. Reverend Lucius Walker to visit Cuba. This proposal, encouraged by Sandinista Sergio Arce, materialized a short time later. At that time, Pastors for Peace provided aid and solidarity to Nicaragua and El Salvador. Reverend Walker made a second trip to Cuba with the purpose of finding ways in which his organization could help the Cuban people. He believes there is a close relationship between the teachings of the Book of Esther and the struggle against the U.S. economic blockade of Cuba. According to him:

> I think it is important for Christians to practice their faith. As Christians we have the vision of a new society and therefore it is our responsibility to help build that society. It is a revolutionary task and also proof of how we can make a dream come true, freeing the oppressed, giving them new hope and strength. Cuba is an example, it is a light in the universe and we must help it stay that way.[118]

Further on he revealed that:

> The United States is not a Christian nation. I believe that each country should exercise freedom of religion, letting their citizens practice the faith they choose; however, in the United States, capitalism as a system has led to the prevalence of an attitude of greed and the predominance of personal power, which has become stronger than the disposition toward love and of sharing with your neighbor, the basic principles of the Christian faith.[119]

118. Annet Cárdenas. "Lucius Walker: Evangelios de paz" (Lucius Walker: Gospels of Peace). *Bohemia* magazine, October 28, 1994, 11. (Retranslated from Spanish.)
119. Ibid.

Indeed, for any person who considers himself a Christian, the economic blockade of Cuba, as well as the invasions and aggressions successive U.S. administrations have been carrying out for two centuries with the aim of plundering and pillaging are immoral and contrary to religious faith.

Referring to the magnitude of the solidarity with Cuba movement in the United States, Reverend Lucius Walker stated:

> In the United States, the Venceremos Brigade, the Information Party, the International Solidarity with Cuba Group, the Hands Off Cuba Movement, Global Exchange and many other organizations came together and worked shoulder to shoulder with us to say No! to the empire's evil doings.[120]

Members of the Episcopal Fellowship and Brotherhood Churches, Jewish Synagogues, the Baptist National Convention of the United States, and the Committee for Social Justice, along with many other organized or independent honest U.S. citizens, have joined together with the Pastors for Peace in their efforts to help Cuba.

Pastors for Peace categorically refuses to ask the Treasury Department for licenses to send aid to Cuba, because this would legitimize an economic blockade they consider to be illegal and immoral. It is, therefore, the U.S. people who are unmasking the hypocrisy of Washington's governing circles, who call themselves Christians and democrats.

As Fidel Castro has said: "There are 10,000 times more coincidences between Christianity and Communism than between Christianity and capitalism."[121] The Revolution did away with theft, embezzlement and corruption and the Church preaches that we should not steal. The Revolution noticeably decreased

---

120. Lucius Walker. Speech given at the Martin Luther King Jr. Center, in *Granma* daily, December 1, 1992, 7. (Retranslated from Spanish.)
121. Frei Betto. Op. cit., 13.

both infant mortality and maternal mortality, raised the average life expectancy and cultivated human solidarity among men and women both within and beyond Cuba's borders, and the Church preaches, "love thy neighbor as thyself." Cuban society has been educated in the ethical and moral principle of respect for the family and women. One of the Church's commandments says "Thou shalt not covet thy neighbor's wife." The Revolution combats deceit and lies, which the Church also condemns.

In his conversation with Frei Betto, Fidel Castro said: "When the Church fosters the spirit of self-sacrifice and the spirit of austerity, and when the Church urges humility, we have exactly the same thing in mind when we say that it is a revolutionary's duty to be self-sacrificing and live modestly and austerely."[122]

As an example of this, he mentioned the work carried out by nuns, and stressed that what they do is what would be expected of communists; by caring for people suffering from leprosy, tuberculosis and other kinds of contagious diseases, they are doing what would be expected of communists. He added that people who are dedicated to an ideal, to their work, and are capable of self-sacrifice, are precisely what a communist should be.

Life has demonstrated that the strategic—not tactical—character of unity among Christians and Marxists put forth publicly for the first time in 1971 by President Fidel Castro in Chile was a key proposition. The fruits of this can be seen now when many believers in the world are in agreement with the Cuban process.

The enemies of the poor, whether they be disguised as democrats or Christians, are extremely powerful, and to overcome them there must be unity among all the world's poor. If up to now they have overcome us with their tactic of dividing us into believers and nonbelievers, whites and blacks, citizens of one country and citizens of another, our tactic should be one of unity.

122. Ibid, 184.

The reason for this book is to report on what is deliberately not said about Cuba, to compare the successes of its system—condemned to be ignored by the mass media controlled by its bitterest enemies—with the reality lived by millions of human beings in the Third World and the developed countries, especially in the United States, and to demonstrate that there exists another way of achieving our countries' development. We cannot claim that the path chosen by Cuba has been an easy one, or free of errors, but the Cuban people have had the capacity to reflect on these, to combat and overcome them.

It is true that purchasing fuel-wasting public transit vehicles from socialist East European countries could be qualified as a great economic error under normal circumstances. But faced with the impossibility of access to the Western market, because of both the economic blockade and the absence of credits in that world, Cuba had no other alternative but to get its supplies from the East so the country wouldn't come to a standstill. We could say the same thing concerning the acquisition of certain technology; it may not have been the best, but it was all that was available.

The Cuban leadership itself criticized the imitation of foreign models, as well as the paternalism and egalitarianism, among other phenomena, which proved to be so harmful.

The hypocrisy behind the criticisms and accusations leveled against Cuba is clearly reflected by the fact that the Western world and the United States, far from lending Cuba a helping hand to overcome its underdevelopment, did everything in their power to asphyxiate the Revolution right from its beginnings. Therefore, it is impossible to speak of errors if we isolate the Cuban process from the historical context and its interrelation with other countries, in particular the United States.

Independently of the tactical errors committed by the Cubans in meeting their goals, they have achieved an impressive level of economic independence. Cuba can boast an infinite number of achievements in other spheres, but readers should already have sufficient information to judge for themselves.

Never before has a people been more aware of its aspirations, never ever has a people been better informed of the motives for its struggles, its programs, its perspectives, its successes and its failures. At all congresses—of children, youth, students, workers, women, etc.—held in Cuba, the country's highest leadership participates actively with the purpose of responding to or resolving problems, concerns and needs, or simply to gather information from those assembled, who are the representatives of each and every member of their organizations.

As a development model the Cuban system has contributed— and can contribute even more—to the rest of the world: its achievements; methods to reach new goals; its work style; the dialectical way in which it deals with the need to adapt to international reality—without compromising its strategies or renouncing its achievements—in order to insert itself in the international economy and commerce; its opening to foreign capital while maintaining a nationalist policy, yet without falling into ridiculous chauvinism; and the close links between the people and the government. All these factors make Cuba what *The New York Times* calls a "political curiosity."

Reality has demonstrated that this "Soviet colony" or "Moscow's satellite", as the hostile reactionary press used to refer to Cuba, has become one of the world's most independent and sovereign countries—in spite of the incredible conditions in which it must make its way—thanks to its intransigence in the defense of universal principles which have benefitted every country in the world, and especially the smallest ones.

We are convinced that Cuba has made one of the greatest contributions ever to the world: it has demonstrated that with a capitalist model based on selfishness, it is impossible to resolve the grave problems faced by humanity. The Cuban people are showing us that there is a more humane and effective way of achieving this goal.

BIBLIOGRAPHY

BOOKS

ALEMANY Y BOLUFER, JOSÉ. *Nuevo diccionario de la lengua española* (New Dictionary of the Spanish Language), Barcelona: Editorial Ramón Sopena S.A., 1961.

CLINTON, BILL AND GORE, AL. *The People Come First.* Retranslated from a translation by Ana I. Stellino. Mexico: Editorial Diana México, 1993.

Constitution of the Republic of Cuba, Editora Política publishers. Havana: 1994.

FEDERATION OF CUBAN WOMEN. *Informe Central al VI Congreso de la Federación de Mujeres Cubanas* (Main Report to the 6th Congress of the Federation of Cuban Women): Havana, 1995.

FERNÁNDEZ-RUBIO, ÁNGEL. *Instrumentos jurídicos internacionales* (International Legal Instruments), vols. 2 and 3, Havana: Editorial Pueblo y Educación, 1991.

FONER, PHILIP S. *Our America.* New York-London: Monthly Review Press, 1997.

FREI BETTO. *Fidel & Religion. Conversations with Frei Betto.* Ocean Press publishers, 1990.

LARRAZÁBAL, FELIPE. *La vida y correspondencia general del Libertador Simón Bolívar* (The Life and Correspondence of the Liberator Simón Bolívar), 5th ed., New York: El Espejo y Cedar Street print shop, 1847.

MARTÍ, JOSÉ. *Obras completas* (Complete Works), vols. 1 and 4, 2nd ed., Havana: Editorial de Ciencias Sociales, 1975.

MINISTRY OF CULTURE. *Algunos datos sobre la gestión cultural actual* (Some Facts on Current Cultural Activities), Havana: 1991.

Playa Girón: derrota del imperialismo (The Bay of Pigs: A Defeat for Imperialism), vol. 4, Havana: Ediciones Revolución, 1962. Vol. 4.

Webster's New Collegiate Dictionary, Springfield: G. & C. Merriam Co. Publishers.

World Almanac 1968. Printed in the United States of America by St. Ives, Inc. 2025 McKinley St., Hollywood, Fl., America Publishers, 1967.

World Almanac 1994. Printed in the United States of America by St. Ives, Inc. 2025 McKinley St., Hollywood Fl., America Publishers, 1993.

ARTICLES

AVENDAÑO PÉREZ, BÁRBARA. "La tuberculosis no admite perder tiempo" (Tuberculosis Can't Wait), in *Tribuna* newspaper. Havana, July 17, 1994.

BAÉZ DELGADO, LUIS. "Carta pública a un presidente" (Open Letter to a President), in *Granma* daily. Havana, June 2, 1994.

CANO, LEONARDO. "Amos de imágenes y palabras" (Masters of Images and Words), in *Granma* daily. Havana, August 8, 1994.

CÁRDENAS, ANNET. "Lucius Walker: Evangelios de paz" (Lucius Walker: Gospels of Peace), in *Bohemia* magazine. Havana, October 28, 1994.

CARRASCO MARTÍN, JUANA. "Vericuetos de una manipulación" (The Rough Tracks of Manipulation), in *Bohemia* magazine. Havana, March 19, 1993.

CASTRO RUZ, FIDEL. Speech at meeting with Pastors for Peace, in *Granma* daily. Havana, December 13, 1992.

CINCOTTA, HOWARD. *¿Qué es la democracia?* Retranslated from translation by Ángel Carlos González. U.S. Information and Cultural Service, November 1991.

CLARO, ELSA. "Un mundo ancho y ajeno" (A Wide and Foreign World), in *Bohemia* magazine. Havana, March 19, 1993.

"Condena presidente de juristas americanos bloqueo a Cuba" (President of American Jurists Condemns Blockade of Cuba), in *Granma* daily. Havana, September 2, 1994.

"Crisis educacional en Venezuela" (Educational Crisis in Venezuela), in *Granma* daily. Havana, March 3, 1994.

"Cuba es un ejemplo en materia social" (Cuba Is an Example in Social Context), in *Granma* daily. Havana, June 16, 1994.

"Cuba hoy", in *Bohemia* magazine. Havana, October 14, 1994.

"Departamento de Estado a tribunales por negar visa a músicos cubanos" (Lawsuit Against State Department for Denying Visas to Cuban Musicians), in *Granma* daily. Havana, May 25, 1994.

DÍAZ, NIDIA. "Motivación económica con ropaje político" (Economic Motivations in Political Clothing), in *Granma* daily. Havana, September 2, 1994.

DUFFLAR AMEL, JUAN. "Estados Unidos implantó en Guatemala el primer plan neofascista en el continente" (United States Established in Guatemala First Neo-fascist Plan in the Continent), in *Trabajadores* newspaper. Havana, June 27, 1994.

"Enviará Estados Unidos a emigrados ilegales a la base yanqui de Guantánamo" (U.S. to Send Illegal Immigrants to Guantanamo Naval Base), in *Granma* daily. Havana, August 20, 1994.

GAINZA, MIGUEL A. "¿Le da vergüenza, Presidente?" (Aren't You Ashamed, Mr. President?), in *Sierra Maestra* newspaper. Santiago de Cuba, August 6, 1994.

HERNÁNDEZ, RAFAEL. "La bola de cristal fracturada" (The Broken Crystal Ball), in *Juventud Rebelde* weekly. Havana, October 2, 1994.

"Impide EE.UU. traslado de 500 deportistas de varios países a Cuba" (U.S. Hampers Cuba Tour of 500 Athletes from Various Countries), in *Granma* daily. Havana, April 20, 1994.

"Inaugurado Biotecnología '94" (Biotechnology '94 Inaugurated), in *Granma* daily. Havana, November 29, 1994.

"Indice de alfabetizados en Cuba, vergüenza para Estados Unidos" (Literacy Rate in Cuba, Humiliation for the United States), in *Granma* daily. Havana, February 24, 1994.

LAGE, CARLOS. Television appearance on the program "Hoy Mismo, in *Granma* daily. Havana, November 10, 1992.

"La lista negra de Washington" (Washington's Blacklist), in *Bohemia* magazine. Havana, August 19, 1994.

LEÓN COTAYO, NICANOR. "La mujer en Estados Unidos" (Women in the United States), in *Trabajadores* newspaper. Havana, July 18, 1994.

_____. "¿Quién manda en Estados Unidos?" (Who's in Charge in the United States), in *Granma* daily. Havana, July 23, 1994.

"Ley No. 72. Ley electoral" (Law No. 72. Electoral Law), in *La Gaceta Oficial de la República de Cuba*. Havana, November 2, 1992.

MARTÍNEZ CORONA, CONRADO. "Compartimos con nuestro pueblo la alegría de habernos ubicado en el quinto puesto" (We Share with Our People the Joy of Winning 5th Place), in *Granma* daily. Havana, August 12, 1992.

MARTÍNEZ, SILVIA. "Invierte Cuba 4,3 millones de pesos cada 24 horas en la seguridad social" (Cuba Invests 4.3 Million Pesos Every 24 Hours in Social Security), in *Granma* daily. Havana, June 10, 1994.

MÁRQUEZ CASTRO, RENÉ. "Rediseño de la política social cubana" (Cuban Social Policy Redesigned), in *Bohemia* magazine. Havana, November 11, 1994.

MOLINA, ROBERTO. "Abrumadora mayoría aprueba resolución contra el bloqueo" (Overwhelming Majority Approves Resolution Against Blockade), in *Granma* daily. Havana, October 27, 1994.

MONTERO ACUÑA, ERNESTO. "¿Para quién?" (For Whom?), in *Trabajadores* newspaper. Havana, October 31, 1994.

_____. "¿Cima o cisma?" (Peak or Pit?), in *Trabajadores* newspaper. Havana, December 12, 1994.

"Opina congresista que EE.UU. está en camino de convertirse en oligarquía" (Congressman States U.S. is on the Way to Becoming an Oligarchy), in *Granma* daily. Havana, July 30, 1994.

OSA, JOSÉ A DE LA. "Ficción hecha realidad" (Fiction Come True), in *Granma* daily. Havana, February 13, 1993.

_____. "14 meses sin sarampeón" (14 Months Without Measles), in *Granma* daily. Havana, September 15, 1994.

PELÁEZ, ORFILIO. "Uso de delfines en tratamiento para niños" (Dolphin Therapy for Children), in *Granma* daily. Havana, August 27, 1994.

PELL CLAIRBORNE AND LEE HAMILTON. "The Embargo Must End", in *The Washington Post,* September 8, 1994. Retranslated from Spanish.

PRADA, PEDRO. "El laberinto del minotauro" (The Labyrinth of the Minotaur), in *Bohemia* magazine. Havana, August 19, 1994.

_____. "Bloqueo, almas en cerco" (The Blockade, Souls Under Siege), in *Granma* daily. Havana, May 25, 1994.

"Revés en el Senado para plan económico de Clinton" (Senate Setback for Clinton's Economic Plan), in *Granma* daily. Havana, April 23, 1993.

ROBREÑO, GUSTAVO. "Realismo bajo la cúpula" (Realism Under the Top Leadership), in *Granma* daily. Havana, March 19, 1994.

SIMEÓN NEGRÍN, ROSA ELENA. "Retos que enfrentamos" (The Challenges We Face), in *Bohemia* magazine. Havana, November 11, 1994.

SUÁREZ, RAÚL. Author's interview with Reverend Raúl Suárez, head of the Martin Luther King Jr. Center and deputy to the National Assembly of People's Power, January 1995.

"Top Secret", in *Granma International*, Havana, March 16, 1994.

TORRES, HORTENSIA. "Cuba campeón latinoamericano en Juegos para Ciegos y Débiles Visuales" (Cuba, Latin American Champion in Games for the Blind and Visually Impaired), in *Granma daily.* Havana, September 29, 1994.

"Un millón de niños muere anualmente" (One Million Children Die Every Year), in *Granma* daily. Havana, September 1, 1994.

VALDÉS MARÍN, ROLANDO. "Ganan 60 medallas pacientes del Hospital Psiquiátrico" (Psychiatric Hospital Patients Win 60 Medals), in *Juventud Rebelde* weekly. Havana, October 2, 1994.

VÁZQUEZ RAÑA, MARIO. Interview granted by Carlos Lage, secretary of the Executive Committee of the Council of Ministers, to *El Sol de México,* in *Granma* daily. Havana, May 29, 1993.

WALKER, LUCIUS. Speech given at the Martin Luther King Jr, Center, in *Granma* daily. Havana, December 1, 1992.

WATSON, ALEXANDER. Speech given before the Cuban American National Foundation. Retranslated from Spanish.

WATTS, MICHAEL. *¿Qué es una economía de mercado?*, U.S. Information and Cultural Service. Retranslated from Spanish.

NEWS DISPATCHES

AFP. New York, March 19, 1993.

ANSA. Washington, March 17, 1994.

AP. Washington, August 19, 1994. Retranslated from Spanish.

NOTIMEX. Miami, January 31, 1994.

NOTIMEX. San Antonio, June 11, 1994.

PL. Havana, September 26, 1994.

This edition was printed in the Osvaldo Sánchez
printing complex in May, 1997.